Maurizio Canforini

ROME
little Grand Tour

translated by
Veronica Galbiati

Intra
Moenia
edizioni

Rome
little Grand Tour

by Maurizio Canforini

Photo Shutterstock / Alamy

ISBN 9788874212750
© Edizioni Intra Moenia 2023

Il Distico Srl
Via Costantinopoli 94, 80138 – Napoli
www.intramoenia.it – info@intramoenia.it

Graphic design and page layout: Giuseppe Madonna
Cover image: Roman Forum seen from Campidoglio, photo ©Shutterstock;
View of St. Peter's from the garden of the Grand Priory of the Order of the
Knights of Malta, photo ©Shutterstock.

Oh Rome! My Country! City of the Soul!

GEORGE GORDON BYRON

Villa Borghese

The evocative backdrop to the start of this tour inside Villa Borghese is the imposing *Galleria Nazionale di Arte Moderna* ('National Gallery of Modern Art') seen from the top of Piazzale Ferdowsi, the large plaza adjacent to the entrance to the *Giardino del Lago*. The latter serves as the main entrance to the Villa.

Giardino del Lago

*Giardino del Lago i*s known as the 18th-century extension of the Villa, the origin of which can be traced back to at least a century earlier, on 16 May 1605 to be exact, when Camillo, a member of the Borghese family, ascended to the papal throne as Paul V.

This enabled the family to consolidate an extended area of vineyards and a variety of other properties, all located in the vicinity of an old plot of land near the Muro Torto. The main instigator of this enterprise was Scipione Borghese Caffarelli, the Pope's nephew and renown patron of the arts.

That the *Giardino del Lago* is different from the rest of the Villa becomes immediately apparent upon crossing the entrance at *Arco di Settimio Severo*.

Fret not, for this is not a relocation of the famous Roman Forum arch, rather - and much more simply - one of the many fake antiques that populate this site. After all, *Giardino Del Lago* is a pre-romantic garden, in which the blurred boundaries between nature and ruins create a consistent, coherent unity that is preferred to and in contrast with the perfection of Renaissance symmetry. This results, among other things, in

The lake at Villa Borghese with the Temple of Aesculapius in the background. The latter was built at the end of the 18th century by Antonio Asprucci.

surprising scenic effects. The credit for this garden goes to Antonio Asprucci, assisted by Luigi Canina.

Past the *Arco di Settimio Severo* and along the unpaved path of the Orangery (*Aranceria*), on our left our attention will be caught by the pretty lake, which on sunny days is brimming with tourists and couples eager to glide across it on rowing boats. Surrounding them is the squawking of the ducks, other undisputed protagonists of this place. The pond's golden age can be traced back to the Art Nouveau period, i.e. the late 19th and early 20th century, when Queen Elena herself could be spotted here.

Past the lake and being careful not to get run over by rickshaws and electric scooters on the loose, we continue along the avenue, bordering on our right the *Casina dell'Aranciera*, originally called the Casina del Murto Torto, which was irreparably damaged by French cannonade in 1849, during the last, heroic days of the Roman Republic.

Lord Byron
The monument to Byron in the paths of Villa Borghese. While in Rome, the poet said: "Rome is a city of the soul, it is a feeling more than a place".

Having reached the end of Viale dell'Aranciera, we step outside the perimeter of the *Giardino*, finding ourselves on Viale Pietro Canonica, right in the heart of Villa Borghese. It is a sudden switch from the 18th to the 17th century, with the avenues laid out in geometric perfection. We go left and then take the first on the right, and soon find ourselves passing by the *Casina di Raffaello* which, despite its name, has no historical link to the famous painter from Urbino and instead was once the home of the Guardaroba. It is now a toy library.

Continue straight ahead for a short while and you will come across the former Casina delle Rose, now *Casa Del Cinema*, on your right. Here, do not miss the chance to

The statue of Pauline Borghese in the Galleria Borghese. The work is by Canova and is dated 1805. The sitter is portrayed posing as Venus Victorious.

stop in front of the Byron Monument, a replica of the one designed by Bertel Thorvaldsen for Trinity College, Cambridge. The Byron Memorial Appeal chose to commemorate him here too, although the writer's time in Rome was only brief - brief, but not insignificant, so much so that he himself wrote:

"Rome is a city of the soul, it is a feeling more than a place."

Galleria Borghese

Agreeing wholeheartedly with his words, we resume our walk along Viale del Museo Borghese until we reach the building that hosts the Galleria Borghese, one of the city's most beautiful museums. The building dates back to the 17th century and was commissioned by the aforementioned Scipione Borghese Caffarelli, who can be admired in this very museum, portrayed in marble by the skilful hand of Gian Lorenzo Bernini. The Gallery is truly a treasure trove of art, there are so many works here which have shaped the history of art, that choosing just a few to talk about in more detail proves to be a daunting task.

Let us try anyway. Art historian Philippe Daverio asserted that to fully enjoy a museum, one should only dwell on one work of art per visit. We attempt to triplicate his advice. Our first stop will be in front of the sculpture of Pauline Borghese by Canova. Napoleon's sister is immortalised in the nude, lying on her side and posing as Venus Victrix, complete with apple in her hand. The work was created in 1805, when she was barely twenty-five years old and at the height of her beauty. The sculpture was a private gift to her husband Camillo Borghese, whom she wed on her second marriage and betrayed with Swiss punc-

Villa Medici
The 17th-century Villa Medici building is home to the Galleria Borghese, one of the city's most beautiful museums.

Caravaggio's 'David with the Head of Goliath'. Painted in Naples in the last year of his life, the painter portrayed himself in the severed head of Goliath.

tuality. Although made for Camillo's personal pleasure, the sculpture was soon renowned all over Rome. There was even an illicit market for paid admissions, with people secretly bribing the servants of the House of Borghese to be able to sneak in and admire it.

A couple of rooms after *Pauline Borghese* we find ourselves facing yet another sculptural masterpiece, Gian Lorenzo Bernini's *Apollo and Daphne*. In this work, the artist catches the moment in which Apollo, struck by Eros's golden arrow and therefore hopelessly in love with her, is about to grasp Daphne, herself previously struck by Eros's own lead-tipped arrow and therefore horrified at the idea of union with the god, and already becoming a laurel tree. It was she who had desperately pleaded with her father Peneus for just this outcome.

"The hair stretches out into foliage, the arms into branches, the foot, just before so swift, remains nailed down by idle roots", writes Ovid in the Metamorphoses. This sculptural group was completed in the three years between 1622-1625. The following is Canova's judgement when he saw it: *"Group worked with such delicacy that it seems unthinkable, the laurel leaves are of marvellous craftsmanship, beautiful is also the nude which I did not expect so much"*. Bernini himself, seeing the work again forty years later, was impressed by his own handling of the marble at such a young age.

The third stop of the tour, again on the first floor of the palace, is reserved to Caravaggio's *David with the head of Goliath*, a work created in the last years of the painter's life (1609-1610). The painting was presented in absentia by Caravaggio to the papal court, along with a plea for the

Apollo and Daphne
The masterpiece by sculptor Gian Lorenzo Bernini. It captures the moment Daphne is about to turn into a laurel plant.

A glimpse of the Pincio with the panoramic view in the background. The Pincio is a 19th-century addition to the Villa Borghese, created by Giuseppe Valadier and commissioned by Pius IX.

annulment of the death sentence that had been handed to him for slaying Ranuccio Tommasoni in a duel in 1606. Caravaggio portrayed himself in Goliath's severed head and this artistic choice unfortunately proved to be premonitory. Indeed, the pardon was granted, but never reached the painter who died on the beach in Porto Ercole in the same year, 1610.

Pincian Hill

Once outside the museum, we retrace our steps towards *Il Pincio* ('Pincian Hill'), the final destination of our walk. To get there, we pass by the impressive *Fontana dei Cavalli Marini* ('Fountain of the Sea Horses') and, walking along Piazza di Siena from above, we find ourselves back on Viale Pietro Canonica. To our right, somewhat hidden by vegetation, is the *Gigi Proietti Globe Theatre*, an Elizabethan and Shakespearean theatre par excellence. Built in 2003, it perfectly replicates the original and every summer stages the Bard's plays to great acclaim, especially among young audiences. We leave it to the sound of the incipit of a sonnet that the great Gigi Proietti, unforgettable artistic director of this little gem, dedicated to the theatre:

Fontana dei Cavalli Marini
The avenues of the Pincio are graced by numerous fountains.
The Fountain of the Sea Horses stands in the centre of one of Villa Borghese's busiest avenues. It is a late 18th century sculpture commissioned by Prince Marcantonio IV Borghese.

> *Long live the Theatre*
> *Where everything is make-believe*
> *But nothing is fake*
> *And this is true...*

At the end of Viale Pietro Canonica, perhaps after stopping for a drink at one of its distinctive fountains, and past Piazzale delle

Viale Pietro Canonica in Villa Borghese. It is adjacent to the Giardino del Lago and runs alongside the Gigi Proietti Globe Theatre.

Canestre, we get to the Pincio. It is a 19th-century acquisition of the villa. Once called Colle Horticolorum, this public promenade saw the light in 1810 at the hands of architect Valadier and at the behest of Pius VII and his right-hand man, Cardinal Consalvi.

One of the distinctive features of the Pincian Hill's tree-lined avenues is the presence of more than 200 busts. Who had them installed? It was a decision of the glorious Roman Republic government of 1849. Busts were to be erected dedicated to the great personalities of the new Italy. The triumvirate (Saffi, Armellini, Mazzini) allocated 10,000 lire at the time. The task was entrusted to a number of unemployed painters and sculptors: the former were to copy the faces of the chosen characters from well-known paintings, the latter were to sculpt them in marble. Using this method, 52 busts were produced, but they ended up gathering dust in the city's warehouses, given the premature end of the Republican experience. Ironically, it was the arch-enemy of the Republic, Pope Pius IX, who had them installed on the Pincian Hill. Not all of them, however, were agreeable to the papal ideology, and some managed to ascend to the heights of the Hill by changing their appearance in the process, as prescribed by Count Luigi Antonelli:

"They will be reduced to other likenesses and placed on the site, varying in appearance and denomination".

Thus, for example, Vittorio Alfieri became Vincenzo Monti and Macchiavelli became Archimedes.

Among all the busts, there is a very peculiar one. It is that of the astronomer Secchi, whom we visit on Viale del Belvedere, which we access via Viale di Villa Medici.

Fontana dei Satiri
It's one of the many fountains that adorn Villa Borghese. It dates back to 1929 and represents two Satyrs playing with their baby.

View of Rome from Viale del Belvedere. Recognisable, Looking from left to right, are the domes of San Carlo ai Catinari, Sant'Andrea della Valle and San Carlo al Corso.

Why peculiar?

Firstly because through a small hole made in the plinth passes the meridian of Rome, measured by means of a graduated tablet placed precisely on a tree following the indication of the observatory of the Collegio Romano and represented by the opening of a window shutter. Secondly, because he is lucky enough to enjoy every day one of Rome's finest sights: the view from Viale del Belvedere.

Rome from Viale del Belvedere

As we approach the balustrade, we have the feeling of having the whole of Rome at our feet. How do we find order in this thicket of churches and secular palaces that stand before our eyes?

Easily: still facing the balustrade, we turn our head 90 degrees to the left. In this way, our gaze will meet the two towers of the church of the Santissima Trinità ai Monti. From this point, as we gradually turn our gaze to our right, we can admire, in order, the following buildings: the *Quirinale* ('Quirinal Palace'), the *Vittoriano* ('Monument to Victor Emmanuel II'), the *church of Gesù*, the *church of Sant' Ignazio*, the *Gazometro*, the bell tower of *Palazzo Montecitorio*, the *Colosseo Quadrato* and the *Basilica of Santi Pietro e Paolo* at Eur, the *Pantheon Dome*, the church of *Sant'Andrea della Valle*, the helicoidal dome of *Sant'Ivo alla Sapienza*, the *church of Santi Ambrogio e Carlo* al Corso, the *church of Sant'Agnese in Agone*, the *Fontanone del Gianicolo* and, last but not least, the *dome of St. Peter's*.

Taking a picture of the panorama will be the best way to end this walk.

Tridente

Our itinerary starts from the point through which, for centuries, all who entered Rome coming from the north have passed: Porta Flaminia in Piazza del Popolo. Our illustrious predecessors have been, to name but a few, Stendhal, Goethe, Michelangelo, Caravaggio and Queen Christina of Sweden. Speaking of the latter, the inscription on the inner façade of the gate is dedicated to her famous arrival in the Urbe in 1655: Felice Faustoque Ingressui (May the entrance be auspicious and happy). It is the work of Gian Lorenzo Bernini at the behest of the then Pope Alexander VII Chigi. Moreover, Christina's arrival in Rome was a memorable event, as she had just abjured the Protestant religion, embraced Catholicism and abdicated her kingdom.

Church of Santa Maria del Popolo

Beyond the gate we are already in Piazza del Popolo. On our left we find the church of Santa Maria del Popolo. The origin of the building dates back to the early 1100s when Pope Paschal II had a chapel built at the expense of the Roman people on the spot where, according to legend, Nero's royal burial took place. Hence the appellation Del Popolo. The current appearance of the church is due to a renovation ordered by Sixtus IV at the end of the 15th century and carried out by Baccio Pontelli and Andrea Bregno. Like all Roman churches, it is a veritable treasure trove of Art. Among the many masterpieces we choose three. The first is the Cappella della Rovere, the first on the right aisle. The frescoes are by Pinturicchio, who succeeded in creating an effective trompe-l'œil in the architectural

The interior of Santa Maria del Popolo. The origin of the church can be traced back to the beginning of the 12th century with complete renovation during the 15th century at the hands of Baccio Pontelli.

decoration of the chapel thanks to the grotesques painted in the false pillars and in the window sills. This was the first time they were used in modern painting. Pinturicchio was inspired by the pictorial cycle of the *Domus Aurea*, whose rooms had been discovered around that time.

The second highlight is the Chigi Chapel, located in the left aisle. It was embellished in two stages. First at the beginning of the 16th century, when Agostino Chigi, a wealthy Sienese banker, commissioned Raphael Sanzio to decorate it with frescoes. The painter from Urbino drew inspiration from the Pantheon in his designs for the dome. Just look up to see for yourself. Then, during the 17th century, Pope Alexander VII Chigi ordered Bernini to take care of the walls. On the left wall, the sculptor erected the Sepulchral Monument of Sigismondo Chigi and sculpted the prophet Daniel, while on the right he completed the funeral monument of Agostino Chigi, flanked by the statue of Habakkuk.

The Crucifixion of St. Peter
This work by Caravaggio is kept in the Cerasi Chapel in Santa Maria del Popolo. Painted between 1600 and 1601, it is regarded as a masterpiece for its pictorial lighting effects and rendering of details.

Having admired this Renaissance-Baroque artistic marvel, we head for the third and final stop: the Cerasi Chapel. It is located on the left side of the transept, next to the apse.

At its centre is The Assumption of the Virgin by Annibale Carracci, at the two sides The Crucifixion of Peter and The Conversion of Saul, both paintings by Caravaggio. Merisi came to the decoration

Aerial view of Piazza del Popolo. Recognisable at the top is Porta Flaminia, th obelisk in the centre, the two 'twin' churches at the base.

of this chapel on the long wave of the success he had enjoyed with his Contarelli Chapel in San Luigi dei Francesi. It was 1600 and the patron Cerasi wanted to bring together in his chapel the works of two artists at the pictorial antipodes: the classical Annibale Carracci and the revolutionary Caravaggio.

Cerasi was only lucky enough to see Carracci's altarpiece in person, delivered in early 1601. He died on 3 May of the same year and the two Caravaggio canvases, delivered as per contract at the end of that same month, were rejected by the new patron, who remained anonymous. The Merisi was therefore forced to redo them and those are the ones we can admire today.

Piazza del Popolo

Leaving the church, we set off to our left, to-wards the heart of Piazza del Popolo. The current arrangement of the square is due to Giuseppe Val-adier, who worked on it from 1811 to 1824. In the centre of the square shines, surrounded by the four basins with Egyptian lions, the so-called Flamin-ian Obelisk, a good 23.914 m high. It was erected in Heliopolis in front of the Temple of the Sun by Pharaohs Seti I and Ramesses II around 1200 BC. It was brought to Rome by Augustus, who used it in the dividing barrier (or *spina*) in the Circus Maximus. It was placed here by Sixtus V in 1589.

At the beginning of that same century there was also the fan-shaped opening of the square along the three routes: Via Clementina (today Via del Babui-no), Via Lata (today Via del Corso) and Via Leonina (today Via di Ripetta). This is the so-called Tridente, which gives the name to this itinerary of ours. Of the three streets we choose to take Via del Babuino. In doing so we find ourselves skirting the basilica of Santa Maria

The Flaminian Obelisk
Installed in Piazza del Popolo by Sixtus V in 1589, it is an Egyptian obelisk dating back to 1200 BC and standing an impressive 24 mt high.

A glimpse of Via Margutta, described by Winckelmann as noble simplicity and quiet grandeur. The artists' street par excellence, it is an oasis of tranquillity in the heart of the historic centre.

in Monte Santo, one of the two twin churches of Piazza del Popolo. The other is Santa Maria dei Miracoli, on the corner with via di Ripetta. Actually, the two churches are not the same, as the first is elliptical in shape and the other circular. Santa Maria in Monte Santo was erected in 1662 by order of Alexander VII and completed in 1679 thanks to the work of Bernini and Carlo Fontana. It is more commonly known as the Church of the Artists.

Via del Babuino and Via Margutta

Via del Babuino owes its current name to a statue that stands as a decoration on a fountain on the corner with Via dei Greci, near the Atelier Canova Tadolini. The statue depicts a Silenus so ugly that he resembles a monkey, a baboon in fact -'Babuino' in Roman dialect. It was placed here in 1576 and in past centuries it had the honour of being one of Rome's talking statues, on which witty mottos and salacious satires were posted, subordinate only to the more famous Pasquino.

La fontana del Babuino
The fountain dates back to 1576 and has its centrepiece in a silenus so ugly it looks like a monkey: 'babuino' in Roman dialect.

We only walk a small stretch of Via del Babuino. Shortly after the Hotel de Russie, a luxury hotel beloved by many Hollywood stars sojourning in Rome, we turn to our left onto one of Rome's most picturesque streets: Via Margutta.

Tranquillity and silence are the main characteristics of this place, which has always been a street of art. Federico Fellini and Giulietta Masina lived here, and a plaque also reminds us of Pablo Picasso's passage here in 1917, when he was busy working on the great scenery, costumes and sets

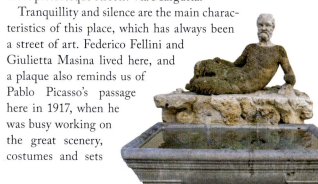

Piazza di Spagna and the Spanish Steps deserted at night. In the foreground the jets of Bernini's Barcaccia.

for the opera Parade, set to music by Satie to a text by Cocteau. At number 51 is the famous house of Roman Holiday, the unforgettable film starring Audrey Hepburn and Gregory Peck. Here, the exhibition of 100 painters is still held every three months. The last stronghold of genuine, non-stereotypical Roman-ness is certainly the Bottega der Marmoraro, with its engraved marble plaques bearing highly philosophical maxims.

Help yourself, that God gave up brings a smile to our faces.

Piazza di Spagna

Having walked the entire street, we return to the last stretch of Via del Babuino, which takes us straight to Piazza di Spagna, Rome's most famous square. It owes its name to the Spanish embassy, now the residence of the Spanish ambassador to the Holy See, which overlooks the square opposite the Immaculate Column. A stop at the Fontana della Barcaccia, opposite the Scalinata di Trinità dei Monti is a must. The fountain is the work of Pietro Bernini, assisted by his son Gian Lorenzo. It was commissioned in 1629 to commemorate the flood of 1598 during which the Tiber overflowed so violently that a boat was swept into the square. The work is a small masterpiece of hydraulic engineering. In fact, since the pressure of the water brought by the Virgin Aqueduct is very low in this location, the fountain's basin is below the surrounding ground and this gives it the gushes and cascades of water typical of Baroque fountains located at higher levels.

The Scalinata (known as the Spanish Steps) came into being 96 years after the construction of the

Roman Holiday
Many films have been shot on this stunning staircase. These include the scene from 'Roman Holiday' with Gregory Peck and Audrey Hepburn.

Via del Corso seen from Piazza Venezia. Formerly known as Via Lata, it is a 1 km long straight street that leads to Piazza del Popolo.

Barcaccia, in 1725 to be precise. It offers a majestic scenography: a double-ramp of curved staircases leading to a wide terrace surrounded by balustrades, from which a succession of other flights of stairs of 12 steps each lead to a total of 138. This is accompanied by the French boundary stones and the eagles of Innocent XIII Conti. The work is by De Santis.

Next to the Scalinata, at number 26 in the square, there is a place worth visiting: the Keats and Shelley Memorial House. The house was the last home of the great English Romantic poet John Keats and is preserved as a tribute to his works and those of his compatriots Percy Bysshe Shelley and Lord Byron, who in Rome found happy inspiration for some of their masterpieces.

Via dei Condotti and Via del Corso

Leaving 26 Piazza di Spagna, we take Via dei Condotti. The street is so called because of the conduits of the Acquedotto Vergine (Virgin Aqueduct) that pass underneath here and reach as far as the Trevi Fountain. A luxury shopping street par excellence, it is also home to the historic Caffè Greco, the oldest café in Rome. The café was founded in 1760 by a certain Nicola della Maddalena, a Venetian by birth and a coffee maker by profession. The Café's Levantine origins can still be seen in the Veduta di Ponte Rialto, a 19th-century work by Ippolito Caffi, which is beautifully displayed in the entrance hall. The café's golden age was during the 19th century, when it was frequented by the most creative minds of the time, including Gogol, Stendhal, Mendelssohn, Schopen-

Caffè Greco
In Via dei Condotti, one must make a stop at the historic Caffè Greco, the oldest in Rome, founded in 1760.

31

Aerial view of Via di Ripetta, one of the three streets of the Tridente. On the right is the Ara Pacis, with the Mausoleum of Augustus opposite.

hauer and Mark Twain. A characteristic feature of the interior is the bric - a - brac on the walls, a tangible sign of the continuous passage over time of artists who often, in bad shape, repaid the owners' hospitality by leaving some of their works as gifts.

At the end of Via dei Condotti, where it meets Largo Goldoni, we cross the Tridente's second street, Via del Corso. It is a 1.5 km long straight stretch connecting Piazza del Popolo with Piazza Venezia. Formerly called Via Lata, it changed its name in 1466 because of the horse races that were held there until the end of the 19th century. If you are a lover of the Grand Tour, then it is a must to stop at number 18 on this street, where the Casa di Goethe is located. Here, under the disguise of the painter Philip Miller, the great German writer lived during his first stay in Rome, from 29 October 1786 until 24 April 1788. In the apartment there is an oil painting depicting the writer life-size against the backdrop of the Roman countryside. It is a 1952 copy by Georgi Takev from the original by Johann Heinrich Wilhelm Tischein, the painter who was Goethe's housemate in this house.

Via di Ripetta, Mausoleo di Augusto and Ara Pacis

Having crossed Via del Corso and taken Via Tomacelli, we soon come to the third of the Tridente streets: Via di Ripetta. This street owes its name to the river port of the same name, rationally arranged in 1705 by the architect Alessandro Specchi. The place name Ripetta, i.e. lower bank, was used to differentiate this harbour from Ripa Grande (Great Bank). Its construction incorporated even the travertines that had fallen from one of the arches of the Colosseum during an earthquake in 1703.

Porto di Ripetta
The street of the same name bordered the ancient river port built in 1705. Ripetta in fact means 'Lower Ripa'.

From where we crossed the street, we can admire the Ara Pacis Augustae a little further to our right, the visit

Detail of the relief decoration of the Ara Pacis, originally polychrome. Its compl[...]tion took three years. The dedication of the altar was celebrated on 30 January 9 B[...]

to which will be the end of this itinerary.

The current arrangement, enclosed in Richard Meier's modern structure that caused so much discussion at the time of its construction, is not the original one. The altar to the Pax Augusta stood in the area of the ancient Campus Martius, together with other monuments wanted by the emperor.

It was approved by the Roman Senate in 13 BC and took three and a half years to complete, with the dedication of the altar celebrated on 30 January 9 BC. Its complex decoration was most likely entrusted to sculptors of Neo-Attic taste active in the 1st century BC. The decorations of the Altar are worthy of an in-depth look, with the reliefs that were originally polychrome. Each of them is a celebration of the work of Augustus, who had brought peace to the Roman people, and served to convey his ideological-political message both to the younger generations, who came to the Campus Martius to train in gymnastic and military exercises, and to anyone who came here to enjoy the natural beauty of the place. In this regard, the Goddess Rome, portrayed seated on the weapons of the vanquished peoples, stands to signify the price of the peace obtained.

Before bidding farewell to this place rich in history and charm, we salute it with a nod.

Ara Pacis
It is an altar built by Emperor Augustus in 9 BC and dedicated to the goddess of Peace.

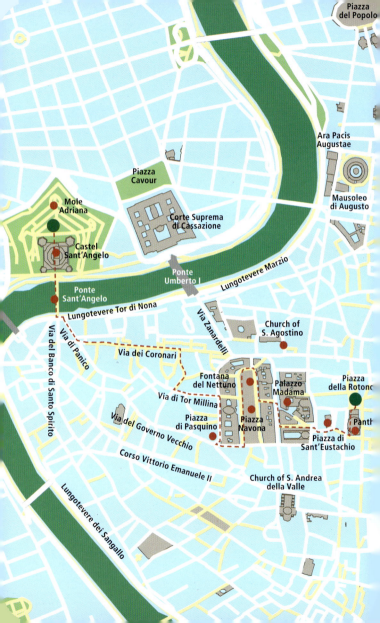

Piazza
del Popolo

Ara Pacis
Augustae

Piazza
Cavour

Mole
Adriana

Corte Suprema
di Cassazione

Mausoleo
di Augusto

Castel
Sant'Angelo

Ponte
Umberto I

Lungotevere Marzio

Ponte
Sant'Angelo

Lungotevere Tor di Nona

Via Zanardelli

Church of
S. Agostino

Via di Panico

Via dei Coronari

Fontana
del Nettuno

Piazza
della Rotond

Via del Banco di Santo Spirito

Via di Tor Millina

Palazzo
Madama

Panth

Via del Governo Vecchio

Piazza
di Pasquino

Piazza
Navona

Piazza di
Sant'Eustachio

Corso Vittorio Emanuele II

Church of S. Andrea
della Valle

Lungotevere dei Sangallo

From the Pantheon to Castel Sant'Angelo

Pantheon

Piazza della Rotonda, with the fountain at its centre, is the beginning of this new itinerary. Until the Renaissance it was a market place. Dominating it is the Pantheon, which is also the Church of Santa Maria ad Martyres. From the centre of the square, we focus on the lintel of the building's façade, which bears the inscription M. AGRIPPA L. COS: TERTIUM FECIT. It refers to the fact that in 27 BC Marcus Vipsanius Agrippa, Augustus' son-in-law and prefect, wanted a temple dedicated to all the gods to be erected on this site. It took two years to build it. It did not originally have the circular appearance it has today, but a rectangular structure. The round layout was acquired between 118 and 125 AD, when Emperor Hadrian, with the help of a couple of fires in the old building, ordered it to be entirely rebuilt. Of the ancient structure, only the lintel with the inscription was retained. A way of preserving the memory of its original patron. The structure consists of a perfect sphere inserted into a cylinder: the height from the floor to the top of the dome measures 43.30m, exactly like its diameter. The famous dome with its circular opening at the top is widely regarded as a marvel of statics. Its creator? There is no certainty, but many believe it to have been the great Apollodorus. The change from *Pantheon* to *Church of Santa Maria ad Martyres* took place on 13 May 609, when Emperor Phocas donated the building to Boniface IV to be turned into a church. The Pope had 28 caskets of Christian martyrs' bones recovered from the catacombs buried here, under the confessional. The *Pantheon* is also a shrine to Art. For example, at the *Altar of the Madonna del Sasso*, is buried

Interior of the Pantheon with its renowned opening in the dome. The structure a perfect sphere inserted in a cylinder: the height from the floor to the top of the dome measures 43.30m, exactly like its diameter.

the great Raphael Sanzio. Engraved on the tomb is Bembo's couplet, which reads: *Here lies Raphael by whom nature, he living, feared to be vanquished and, he dying, to die also.* A curiosity: the bones of the painter from Urbino rested peacefully and blissfully until 14 September 1833, when it was decided to verify whether Raphael had actually been buried there. In this regard, Belli wrote a sonnet full of fierce irony, which began as follows: *It is a ssscene for God, quite a ssscene...*

Leaving the Pantheon, we turn left and soon find ourselves in Piazza Sant'Eustachio. Here we make two stops. The first is in front of the façade of the church of the same name. On top of the gable, a deer's head is on display. This is why the church is an uncommon place for wedding ceremonies [*translator's note*: in Italy, the deer's antlers, and horns in general, symbolize infidelity,]. The second stop we make is on our way to the 83-year-old Caffè Sant'Eustachio, together with the Tazza d'Oro the best known of the historic centre's Modern Cafés. Having sipped our coffee, we head out, turning to our left and, if we look up, we can admire the dome of Sant'Ivo alla Sapienza, unique among all Roman domes. It is helix-shaped and seems to rise over the Palazzo della Sapienza like a waterspout over the sea. The author is the inimitable Borromini. Walking along one of the sides of the La Sapienza building, we find ourselves passing by the graceful Fontana dei Libri (Fountain of the Books). Crossing Corso Rinascimento, we make our triumphal entry into Piazza Navona. The verses of Giuseppe Gioachino Belli accompany us:

'St. Matthew and the Angel' by Caravaggio. It is located in the church of San Luigi dei Francesi, inside the Contarelli chapel. It was the first public commission received by the Lombard painter.

My Piazza Navona has nothing to envy
To St Peter's and Piazza di Spagna.
This is not a square, it's a country
It's a fair, it's a joy...

The square's current appearance is due to the heated rivalry between Bernini and Borromini, both of whom were masterfully exploited by Pope Innocent X and his famous sister-in-law Olimpia Maidalchini. In fact, at the beginning of the 17th century, the square was known as the site of a market. It stood on the site of what had been the Stadium of Domitian, formerly the site of games, Agones in Latin. Hence the square's nickname 'Navona'. In 1644 the turning point: Innocent X, a Pamphilj, ascended to the papal throne and immediately decided to embellish the family palace, which towers over the square and is now the seat of the Brazilian embassy. For this purpose, he teamed up with Rainaldi, his personal architect, with Borromini. During the same period, a competition was also announced for the construction of a fountain in the centre of the square, which was to replace the already existing quadrangular basin used as a drinking trough. Bernini, who was disliked by the Pope as the favourite artist of the predecessor Urban VIII, was excluded from the competition. Subsequently the Pope, disregarding the competition, decided to give the commission to Borromini. He had been convinced by the latter's plan to erect an Egyptian obelisk above the fountain, and on its base four masks would allegorically represent the world's four great rivers: Nile, Ganges, Danube and Rio de la Plata. There was, however, a twist. In 1648, although officially out of the competition, Bernini, at the intercession of

'Madonna of the Pilgrims' by Caravaggio
It is located inside the Basilica of St. Augustine.

41

View of Piazza Navona with the 'Fontana del Nettuno' in the foreground. Further to the right is Borromini's dome of Sant'Agnese in Agone towering over the square.

Donna Olimpia, sent Innocent X a model of the future fountain cast in bronze, which took up Borromini's basic idea in an expanded form. At the sight of the model, the Pope backtracked and definitively entrusted the commission to the Neapolitan sculptor. Borromini was so enraged by the humiliation inflicted on him that he refused to hand over to the enemy the technical data concerning the water supply of the square. In spite of this, Bernini succeeded in getting water to the fountain, so much so that its gurgling sound is recognisable as soon as one sets foot in the square. For what concerns the four statues, if we look at the fountain with the church of Sant'Agnese in Agone directly opposite us, on our right we see the Nile, whose face is covered because its sources were unknown at the time, and on the left the Ganges. If we turn around the fountain and stand with our backs to Sant'Agnese in Agone, to our right we see the Danube, whose face is refined as a representative of cultured Europe, while to our left we find the Rio de la Plata, under whose flank Bernini carved scattered coins, testifying to the natural wealth of those far-off lands.

Fontana del Moro in Piazza Navona
It is located opposite Palazzo Pamphilj, now home to the Brazilian embassy.

Leaving the Fountain of the Four Rivers to its majesty, we cross the square until we reach the corner where it meets Palazzo Braschi. It is just along the walls of the palace that we come to a small widening, Piazza di Pasquino. The name comes from the mutilated torso that is leaning against the wall of Palazzo Braschi. For more than five centuries, Pasquino has been the voice of Rome, hurling his cutting remarks at the constituted power caught up in their criminal contradictions. The most famous talking statue in Rome, with the mottos that anonymous citizens post at its base. It

Fontana dei Quattro Fiumi (Fountain of the Four Rivers). In the foreground i the statue embodying the Ganges. The other three rivers featured are the Nile, th Danube and the Rio de la Plata.

has been in operation since 1501. The statue, of Hellenistic age, was found in the late 15th century in the foundations of Palazzo Orsini and, according to the authoritative opinion of Michelangelo Buonarroti, represents Menelaus carrying the body of the dying Patroclus out of the fray. How did we go from the real Menelaus to the symbolic Pasquino? There are several theories about this, the most credited one seeing Pasquino as a gymnasium teacher who lived just across the street: his pupils, to mock him, named after him this statue, which certainly does not look aesthetically pleasing. Speaking of the famous ones, there's a remark dedicated to Pope Innocent X's sister-in-law, Olimpia Maidalchini, already mentioned in connection to Piazza Navona. About her, he wrote:

Pasquino
The most important and most famous Roman talking statue, it has been in operation since 1501.

Who says woman says harm
Who says female says misfortune
Who says Olimpia Maidachina
Says woman, harm and ruin.

The centuries of Papal Rome were the heyday of Pasquino's witticisms. With the unification of Italy, the quality of the witticisms gradually diminished. Having said goodbye to *Pasquino*, we turn into Via dell'Anima and soon find ourselves in Via della Pace, at the end of which the church of *Santa Maria della Pace* awaits us, its Baroque façade built by Pietro da Cortona. Inside is the remarkable *Chigi Chapel*, whose architecture is attributed to Raphael, author also of the fresco on the archway (Sibyls and Angels). Next to the Church is the *Chiostro del Bramante*, used for temporary exhibitions of great public appeal.

Past the *Arco della Pace*, we get lost in the shady alleys and come to *Via dei Coronari*. Once known

Glimpse of Ponte Sant'Angelo with the Castle in the background. The bridge's ancient name was Elio and it has as many as 12 angels sculpted by Gian Lorenzo Bernini on its sides.

as *Via Recta*, in the Middle Ages it was called Via di Tor Sanguigna, and finally it was named Via dei Coronari because of the sellers of sacred objects, also known as Paternostrari, who stationed themselves in this street because it was an obligatory passage for pilgrims on their way to St Peter's. It measures 500 metres in length. It is considered one of the most beautiful streets in Rome with its Renaissance palaces, including those of Prospero Machi, at number 148, on the wall of which is the following inscription: *Tua puta que tute facis* (Consider yours what you yourself do). On this street is also the oldest of the sacred aedicules in Rome, built in 1523 by Antonio Sangallo the Younger.

Having travelled the entire length of the road in the direction of Via di Panico, we see the destination of this itinerary on our right: *Castel Sant'Angelo*. We reach it by way of the famous bridge, with Bernini's 12 angels towering on its sides. In ancient times the bridge was called Elio. Today's *Castel Sant'Angelo* is nothing more than the reconstruction of the ancient Mausoleum of Hadrian, the tomb that the philosopher emperor wanted built for himself and his successors between 123 and 129 AD. Inside, the ancient 125.50-metre long helicoidal ramp is accessible. This gently sloping ramp wound around the burial cells, completing an entire circumference and overcoming a 12-metre difference in height. Along it passed the funeral procession ascending to the burial chamber located on the first floor of the mausoleum. The Mole Adriana was adapted as a military outpost from the time of Emperor Aurelian (270-275 AD). In 403 Honorius included it in the reinforced city walls and for the first time it was re-

Via dei Coronari
It is 500 metres long and is considered one of the most beautiful streets in Rome.

Interior of Castel Sant'Angelo. It was built between 123 and 129 AD at the behest of Emperor Hadrian, who wanted it as his own Mausoleum.

ferred to as Castellum. In 590 there was the significant event that changed the name to *Castel Sant'Angelo*. It was the time of Gregory the Great and a terrible plague was scourging the city. The Pope thus ordered a penitential procession. When the procession arrived here, headed for St Peter's, legend has it that the archangel Michael was seen hovering in the air in the act of sheathing his sword, as if to signify the imminent end of the pestilence. Therefore, a chapel was built on top of the castle and the place was given this name. The papal influence on the fortress gradually intensified with the construction of the Passetto, an elevated passage which connects the castle directly to the Vatican. This took place in the 13th century.

Once reached the terrace, from where in Puccini's Tosca the protagonist takes mortal flight, we can admire the statue of the archangel Michael. The one we see before us is the seventh angel in chronological order from the 11th century AD that has found a place here. The first was made of wood and ended in decay, the second one in marble was destroyed during an assault on the castle in 1379; it was succeeded by a third one, active until 1453, but this angel too was struck by lightning in 1497. Its replacement, in gilded bronze, was cast in 1527 to make cannons. Then it was the turn of Montelupo's angel, which can now be admired in the Cortile dell'Angelo (Courtyard of the Angel) below. The latter was succeeded in 1752 by the bronze version by Pietro Verschaffelt, which still survives. And it is with his blessing that we ascend the balustrade to enjoy a breathtaking view of the historic centre of Rome.

Statue of Archangel Michael at Castel Sant'Angelo
There have been seven on top of the castle since the 11th century.

Circonvallazione Tri

Via Candia

Viale Sebastiano Veniero

Ottavi

Viale degli Scipioni

Giardini
Vaticani

Santa
Marta

Giardino
Quadrato

Vatican
Museums

Museo Pio
Clementino

Sistine
Chapel

Cortile
della Pigna

St Peter's
Basilica

Viale Vaticano

Via di Porta Cavalleggeri

Via di Porta Angelica

Piazza
San Pietro

Piazza
Risorgimento

Via della Conciliazione

Via Crescenzio

Via Cola di Rienzo

St. Peter's and the Vatican Museums

Piazza San Pietro and the Basilica

Our journey begins in the most famous square in the world: Piazza San Pietro. This masterpiece of monumentality is the work of Gian Lorenzo Bernini, whose intention was to give solemn access to the temple of Christianity, the basilica of the same name. It is an immense ellipse with the two lateral hemicycles consisting of imposing porticos on four rows of columns (284 columns, 88 pillars) supporting an entablature crowned by 140 statues of saints. This is Bernini's celebrated Colonnade, from which we willingly let ourselves be embraced. Afterwards, we take an admiring look at the Egyptian obelisk that stands in the centre and came from Heliopolis. It was found in the Circus of Nero and erected here by Domenico Fontana in 1586. Above it all, however, shines Michelangelo's dome: it has a diameter of no less than 42.56 metres. Finally we decide to enter the basilica. We do so by reaching the portico that stretches the full width of the façade (117 metres).

The structure we see today is the result of the will of Pope Julius II, who in 1505 decided to demolish the old basilica and build a new one. The project was entrusted to Bramante. Julius II died long before the work was completed, also because the St. Peter's Building Site remained open for more than a century and saw as architects, in addition to the aforementioned Bramante, artists of the calibre of Raphael, Antonio Sangallo the Younger, Michelangelo, up to and including Bernini, who experienced one of the darkest moments of his career here due to the demolition of one of the two bell towers planned and intended for the sides of the façade.

Aerial view of Via della Conciliazione, St. Peter's Square and the basilica of the same name. The square has an elliptical shape with the two side hemicycles that are known as the 'Bernini Colonnade'.

Once inside, instead of raising our eyes as would be natural, we lower them in the direction of the floor, which enchants us with its refined designs, the work of talented 16th- and 17th-century masters, Cavalier D'Arpino and Pietro da Cortona above all. There is also an element of the old basilica in the floor: it is an Egyptian red porphyry disc. It is located just beyond the entrance and on it Charlemagne knelt on Christmas night in 800, when Leo III crowned him Emperor of the Holy Roman Empire. These were his official words: *"To Charles, most pious Augustus, crowned by God, great and peaceful Emperor of the Romans, Life and Victory!"*

The Pietà by Michelangelo

Pope Leo III's enthusiasm is ours as we stand at the beginning of the right aisle to admire Michelangelo's Pietà. The Florentine artist sculpted it in 1499, when he was just 23 years old. It is one of the most precious legacies of the old basilica.

It is a pity that it can only be admired from a distance, protected by a glass case. Hired by the then French Cardinal Jean de Bilhères, ambassador of the King of France to the papal court, Michelangelo went to Carrara to choose the best marble and carved the two figures from a single block, a technical virtuosity that was much admired at the time as it was considered to be typical of ancient sculptors. If we rest our gaze on Our Lady's face, we realise that she has a perfect oval and someone at the time pointed out that she was too young to be mother to a 33-year-old son. This is undoubtedly true. The fact is that Michelangelo was so proud of this work that, for the first and only time, he signed it, engraving his name on a sash

Michelangelo's Pietà
The Florentine artist sculpted it in 1499, when he was just 23 years old.

Interior of St Peter's with its famous Baldachin. It is 28.70 metres high. To crea
it, Bernini emptied the Pantheon of all its bronze.

across Mary's chest. Along the right aisle is also the Monument to Christina of Sweden, which was commissioned by Innocent XII. The Queen is instead buried in the Vatican Grottoes. Reaching the space below the dome and raising our eyes, we barely suppress an Oh! of wonder, the same reaction as those who, at this very moment high up on the walkway running around the dome, see us as mere coloured dots in motion. The characteristic of St. Peter's is precisely that it makes its visitors lose their proper sense of proportions and scale. It is no coincidence that Bernini's famous Baldachin does not even seem very tall, although it measures an impressive 28.74 metres in height. It was erected to solve the problem of covering the '*confessione*', which is the semicircular space surrounding the underground Tomb of Peter, and the Basilica's high altar above it. It is a bronze architectural sculpture whose twisted columns bewitch anyone who stops to look at them. To allow Bernini to realise the work, the Pantheon was emptied of its bronze. A controversial decision that made Pasquino pronounce judgement:

The crossed keys
They are St. Peter's emblem.

Quod non fecerunt Barbari
Barberini fecerunt

Translated: What the Barbarians did not do, the Barberini did. The talking statue referred to the family of the then Pope Urban VIII. Among Bernini's collaborators in the completion of the work was a certain Francesco Castelli, who later became known as

Statue of St Peter in the Chair inside the basilica. Long dated to the 5th century AD, it is most probably a 13th century work by Arnolfo di Cambio.

Borromini. Perhaps their rivalry began right here, at St. Peter's, working hand in hand.

Also by Bernini here are the Chair of St. Peter (known as the *Cattedra*), a work of his maturity (1656-1666), commissioned by Alexander VII Chigi, and the sepulchral monument dedicated to the same pope (1671-1681). The latter work is arranged around the door of Santa Marta, which communicates with the outside of the church, and features the statues of Justice and Prudence, as well as the more disturbing statues of death, in addition to the Pope kneeling bareheaded. A curiosity: the Pope died before work on his tomb began, in 1667. This leads us to say that the idea of having a sepulchre erected while he was still alive did not prove auspicious, to the delight of the superstitious.

Before leaving the basilica, let us pay homage in the nave to the statue of the saint to whom this place is dedicated, namely St Peter. *St. Peter in the Chair* is the correct name for the work. It depicts the saint in a seated position, with a blessing hand. For a long time the work was considered to be a 5th century statue. Instead, it is probably a 13th-century work by Arnolfo di Cambio. If we approach the sculpture, we notice that the right foot, protruding, is visibly worn down compared to the left. This is because tradition says it is a devout act to touch it and do the sign of the cross.

Having complied with the tradition, we go outside. Our next target is the *Vatican Museums*.

Tomb of Pope Alexander VII
It is located around the Porta di Santa Marta.

Helicoidal access ramp to the Vatican Museums. The museums belong to the complex of the Vatican Apostolic Palaces.

To reach them, we are compelled to start from the right hemicycle of Bernini's colonnade, then walk along the walls until we enter the slope of Viale Vaticano. It is roughly a quarter of an hour's walk. *The Vatican Museums* belong to the complex of the Vatican Apostolic Palaces and together with the Sistine Chapel are the only ones open to the public. To visit them meticulously would take a lifetime. In this itinerary we opt for the direct route to the Sistine Chapel. Before embarking on it, however, after a short stop on the panoramic balcony, we decide to enter the *Pinacoteca*, commissioned by Pius VI, an art gallery that chronicles the history of Italian painting from the 11th to the 18th century. Inside, one of the obligatory stops is in front of Giotto's *Stefaneschi Triptych* (1315-20).

Its peculiarity is that it was painted on both sides, because it should have been located in the ancient basilica of St. Peter's, on the high altar to be precise, halfway between the pontiff and the faithful, so that everyone could enjoy Giotto's pictorial mastery. Also noteworthy are the *Angelii Musicanti and Teste di Apostoli* (Musician Angels and Heads

Angelo Musicante (Musician Angel) It is a 15th-century work by Melozzo da Forlì.

of Apostoli) by Melozzo da Forlì, a 15th-century artist and official painter of Sixtus IV. Michelangelo used them as inspiration for his work in the *Sistine Chapel*. The icing on the cake of our visit to the Pinacoteca is the room entirely dedicated to Raphael Sanzio. Among the works on display, we choose first of all the *Oddi Altarpiece*, which depicts the Coronation of the Virgin. There is a curiosity in this regard: Raphael has portrayed himself on the far right of the panel in the guise of St James the Lesser. The work comes from the church of *San Francesco al Prato* in Perugia, where it was originally placed. We end our presence here

The bronze Pinecone in the courtyard of the Vatican Museums. The author is Publius Cinius Salvia and in Roman times it stood in Campo Marzio, as a fountain decoration.

by admiring the majestic central canvas, *The Transfiguration*, dated 1519, in all probability the final work of Raphael, who would shortly thereafter die prematurely.

Outside the Pinacoteca, we come to the Cortile della Pigna (Pinecone Courtyard), where a bronze pinecone towers, whose author is Publius Cinius Salvia, and which originally stood in Campo Marzio, where it decorated a fountain by spurting water from the tips of the scales. It also impressed Dante, who wrote in the thirty-first canto of the Inferno: *"His face seemed to me as long and thick as the Pinecone of St Peter's in Rome"*.

At this point we retrace our steps, even though a visit to the *Pio Clementino Museum* would have afforded us the sight of two sculptural masterpieces: the *Apollo of Belvedere* and the *Laocoön* group. We head straight for the Sistine Chapel. A delicious appetiser, however, is provided by the *Raphael Rooms*. There are four rooms under this heading and they were meant to be Julius II's new private quarters, the decoration of which was commissioned to the painter in 1508. Neither the patron nor the painter got to admire the finished work: Julius II passed away in 1513 and Raphael in 1520. The rooms were completed in 1524, under Clement VII, by the workshop of the Urbino painter, particularly Giulio Romano and Francesco Penni. The rooms overlook the Cortile del Belvedere on one side and the narrow, fortified Cortile del Pappagallo on the other. The most famous of the four is certainly the Stanza della Segnatura, whose name derives from the tribunal of the *Segnatura Gratiae et Iustitiae*, the Holy See's highest court, which was presided by the Pope himself and used to

The Laocoön
The sculptural group was unearthed in 1506 in Rome, on the Esquiline Hill.

The vault of the Sistine Chapel. It took Michelangelo four years of hard and solitary work to complete it. It was inaugurated by Julius II on 1 November 1512.

meet in this room. The four frescoes are dedicated to the cornerstones of the ideal order of humanistic culture: Theology, Philosophy, Poetry and Jurisprudence. The absolute masterpiece is the one dedicated to philosophy: The School of Athens. Against the backdrop of classical architecture, great philosophers, mathematicians and other great figures of antiquity are depicted reflecting and dialoguing with each other. To some of these characters, Raphael (who himself is self-portrayed in the fresco at the far right, with his gaze turned towards the public) wanted to give the likeness of some of the great artists of his time, so as to celebrate the very soul of the Renaissance, which stood in direct descent from Greek classicism. Thus Plato, who points to the sky with his hand and stands next to Aristotle, bears the features of Leonardo da Vinci. At the bottom, on the other hand, sitting in total solitude and writing on a block of marble is Heraclitus, with the likeness of Michelangelo Buonarroti.

At this point we cross the threshold of the Chapel, which boasts 41.93 metres in length, 13.41 metres in width and 20.7 metres in height. Before the beginning of Michelangelo's work in 1508, the vault was a simple starry sky. The entire chapel had been built between 1478 and 1481 by Giovannino de' Dolci based on a design by Baccio Pontelli. It was Julius II who convinced Michelangelo to fresco it with episodes from Genesis. It was a titanic undertaking that lasted four years. Suspended on the scaffolding, exposed to the ele-

Michelangelo's masterpiece
A detail of the Creation of Adam, a fresco decorating the vault of the Sistine Chapel.

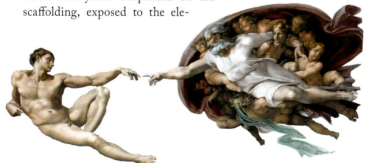

The wall of the Last Judgement. A work of Michelangelo's late maturity. Following the Council of Trent, the 400 nudes were covered by Daniele da Volterra, wh
for this reason was nicknamed 'Braghettone' ('Big Pants').

ments, Michelangelo experimented with every possible position to ease the neck pain that gripped him after hours and hours of uninterrupted painting. The colours dripped into his eyes and made him almost blind. Eventually, despite much agony, he managed to complete his work and on 1 November 1512 all of Rome flocked to the Sistine Chapel for the solemn service officiated by Julius II.

We would never take our eyes off the *The Creation of Adam* scene, with God only having to stretch out his arm towards his son for a breath of his power to bring man and the world into existence. Adam's features are striking with an accentuated bodily power, characteristics that Michelangelo believed to be a sign of the divine. Then, on the wall, *The Last Judgement*, a work of Michelangelo's late maturity, which was commissioned in 1536, when the artist was 61 years old. It took him five years to complete it and show it to Paul III. Its four hundred nudes are sublime, we are left mesmerised by the whirling of the figures around the Son of God, whose features are identical to those of the Adam in the vault, whose arm raised above his head expresses a gesture of vehement and inexhaustible accusation. One really does get the impression that the figures on the wall might suddenly burst out of the wall, grab us and pull us in, Heaven or Hell that is. A demonstration of awe-inspiring vitality, one of the highest artistic and spiritual peaks of Western art of any era.

Detail of the Last Judgement
It took Michelangelo five years to paint the entire fresco.

Janiculum Hill

Despite being located outside the seven mythical hills of Rome, the Gianicolo (Janiculum Hill), is linked to the city's history as much as the traditional ones, to the extent that it is also known as the Ottavo Colle (Eighth Hill). There are two theories on the origin of its name: for some, the term comes from the God Janus (Giano in Italian), a divinity representing beginnings and passage; for others, the origin is to be found in Ianua, a transit gate to Etruria, since the hill and Trastevere were once Etruscan.

Church of San Pietro in Montorio

Our itinerary begins in Piazza San Pietro in Montorio, which is dominated by the church of the same name. It was decided to erect the latter here in the 11th century. It was mistakenly thought that Peter had been crucified here. During the 15th century, the old building was demolished and a new one built. Worthy of admiration inside is the first chapel on the right, Cappella della Flagellazione, frescoed in oils by Sebastiano del Piombo, born Sebastiano Luciani. Why the nickname Del Piombo? It was due to his position as 'piombarote papale', i.e. keeper of the seal to the Papacy, a position Sebastiano obtained in 1531, with the obligation to wear the friar's robe.

"If you saw me monk, I think you would laugh. I am the most handsome friar in Rome. In truth, I do not think so", Sebastiano wrote to Michelangelo Buonarroti on this subject. The latter helped him with the chapel fresco, donating a drawing. It is the Christ at the Column of the Flagellation. The original is kept in the British Museum in London. The altar currently houses the Crucifixion

"Er Fontanone del Gianicolo'. The work of Giovanni Fontana and Flamini Ponzio at the behest of Pope Paul V. Stones from Forum of Nerva were repur posed for its construction.

of St. Peter by Vincenzo Camuccini, based on an original by Guido Reni. It was there in 1523 that Raphael's Transfiguration was placed, which then in 1797 was taken to Paris, only to return to Rome in 1816, but this time to the Pinacoteca Vaticana, as we mentioned earlier.

Fontana dell'Acqua Paola

Returning to the road, we take Via Garibaldi on our right, uphill. Straight away we notice a plaque with a 140 cannon shell from the French artillery, which carried out a heavy bombardment here in 1849, during the heroic months of the Roman Republic. We will talk about these events at a later point. In the meantime, we are going to enjoy the gurgling of the Fontana dell'Acqua Paola, otherwise known as Er Fontanone, located in a widening with a breath-taking view of the city. The structure is elevated on a wide terrace overlooking the street and was built at the behest of Paul V and by Giovanni Fontana and Flaminio Ponzio, who knew how to make the best use of the stones transported here from Forum of Nerva. The fountain is in the shape of a large castle with five niches, the central three of which are adorned with columns from the Roman Forum, while the outer columns belong to the old St. Peter's Basilica, by far the most repurposed of the lost Roman monuments. The large basin on the ground, which gives the fountain its grandeur, was added later. This was in 1690 and it was built by Carlo Fontana at the behest of Alexander VIII. An anecdote: on the day of the final rehearsal, the water gushed out with such force that it broke through the balustrade and tumbled down into the valley. The event did not escape Pasquino's notice:

Tempietto del Bramante It is located in Piazza San Pietro in Montorio in the courtyard of the convent of the same name.

View of Rome from the Gianicolo. Easily recognisable is the Vittoriano, glowing with the splendour of its Botticino marble.

"The miracle is done, O Holy Father, with your water that pleases you so much; but the miracle would be way better if you swapped the water with Orvieto wine".

The place has also been much exploited in movies, including Sorrentino's *The Great Beauty*.

Piazzale Garibaldi and the events of 1849

Having taken in the view, we embark on the leafy Passeggiata del Gianicolo ('Janiculum promenade'), a road flanked by busts of the heroes of the 1849 Roman Republic. Finally, we arrive at the renowned Piazzale Garibaldi. If we were to arrive here exactly at noon, our arrival would be greeted by the unfailing cannon shot, audible throughout much of the historic centre. Dominating the square is the *Monument to Giuseppe Garibaldi*, consisting of several bronze sculptures: an equestrian statue of the hero placed on a large marble pedestal, with allegorical figures of Europe and America sculpted on either side. It was inaugurated on 20 September 1895 and is the work of Emilio Gallori.

Why a square and a statue honouring Garibaldi right here, on the Gianicolo? Because it was here that Garibaldi, in the spring of 1849, fought during the strenuous defence of the Roman Republic. The entire hill is full of mementos of those epic days, as we have already seen at *San Pietro in Montorio*. Let us briefly summarise them. In the middle of 1848, Pius IX's popularity throughout the Papal States was in sharp decline due to his restorative policies and betrayal of the Risorgimento ideals that were simmering across Italy. Eventually, Pius IX exiled himself to Gaeta, in the King-

Cannone del Gianicolo
It fires blanks, every day, at noon sharp.

Monument to Giuseppe Garibaldi on the Gianicolo. It is the work of Emilio Gallori and was unveiled on 20 September 1895. On this hill 'The Hero of Two Worlds' was the protagonist of the ill-fated defence of the Roman Republic.

dom of the Two Sicilies, while the Republic was proclaimed in Rome. Garibaldi immediately moved towards the Urbe. These were days of great patriotic enthusiasm, unfortunately short lived: Pius IX's request for help from other European nations to come to Rome to restore the status quo by force, immediately met the approval of Napoleon III, Emperor of France. The first bombardment by the French, led by General Oudinot, took place on 30 April 1849. The Romans and patriots, who had come here from all over Italy, defended themselves heroically, but without hope. On 2 July, the besiegers entered the city and the glorious experience of the republicans came to an end, but not before leaving to posterity their approved constitution, one of the most enlightened in History.

Among the most illustrious architectural victims of the fighting was *Villa del Vascello*, built in the 17th century by the female architect Plautilla Briccia. On the square stands the '*Casotto dei Burattini*' (Puppet House), which in past centuries was the most popular show watched by children and adults alike. The most famous puppeteer was Gaetano Santangelo, better known as Gaetanaccio, portrayed on stage by the Roman duo Gigi Magni and Gigi Proietti in the comedy of the same name.

Monument to Anita Garibaldi
She was among the female protagonists of the Roman Republic.

Leaving the square and continuing along the Gianicolo promenade, while on our left there is a view of Villa Pamphilj from above, we come across the Monument to Anita Garibaldi, the Brazilian wife of the Hero of the Two Worlds. In this equestrian statue, Anita is depicted riding, pistol in hand, carrying her son Menotti in her lap. She fell ill with malaria during the retreat after the defeat of the Roman Republic, and died shortly after in Ravenna.

Trastevere

Trastevere is the first district established on the right bank of the Tiber. The name derives from the Latin *Trans Tiberim*, 'beyond the Tiber'. Once a hostile area inhabited by the Etruscans, the Romans occupied it to control the river on both sides, but at the time Rome did not count much on owning the area, so much so that it was connected to it by a wooden bridge, the *Sublicio*. Things changed a great deal with the passage of the centuries, first with the patrician villas of the Republican era, then in the Middle Ages with the arrangement of the district in a guise very similar to today's, and with its reputation as the heart of Old Rome. For many, the adjectives Trastevere and Roman are perfectly superimposable.

Basilica of Santa Maria in Trastevere

Our starting point for our walk is *Piazza Santa Maria in Trastevere*, where the basilica of the same name stands, definitely worth a visit. We are welcomed by the 18th-century portico, the work of Carlo Fontana, the last intervention that the church underwent during its two-thousand-year history. *Santa Maria in Trastevere*, in fact, is probably the oldest church in Rome, or at least the first one dedicated to the cult of the Virgin Mary. According to legend, it was founded in the 3rd century AD by Pope Calixtus I, a pontiff with a stormy and controversial biography to say the least, on the site of the Taberna Meritoria, where in 38 BC a miraculous eruption of oil, Fons Olei ('oil wells') took place, which reached as far as the Tiber and was later interpreted as the announcement of the birth of Jesus. It is no coincidence that the building's original name was *Santa Maria Fons Olei*. In the

The interior of the Basilica of Santa Maria in Trastevere. Founded in the 3rd century AD by Pope Callistus I on the site of the ancient Taberna Meritoria, was the first church in Rome consecrated to the cult of the Virgin Mary.

beginning it was a small structure. It became a Basilica under Pope Julius I (337-352), was enlarged by Gregory IV (827-844) to house the bodies of the Saints taken from the catacombs exposed to the Saracen hordes, and was finally rebuilt by Innocent III (1130-1143) with materials removed from the Baths of Caracalla. From the same period is also the beautiful Romanesque

bell tower that stands out above the entire building. The interior has three naves. The central one features a wooden lacunar ceiling designed by Domenichino (1617). The apse is remarkable with its cycle of mosaics and frescoes varying in date and author. The upper ones, dating from the 12th century, have as their subject Innocent II with a model of the church.

Piazza Santa Maria in Trastevere with the basilica in the background The church is probably the oldest in Rome.

Those below, also magnificent, are from the late 13th century and bear the signature of Pietro Cavallini. They depict episodes from the *Life of Mary*. Before we leave the church, we head to the chapel to the left of the altar, protected by the balustrade. At the back, we can admire a 7th-century panel painting, the *Madonna Della Clemenza*, which has the peculiarity of having been successfully painted with the encaustic technique, the same technique that was fatal to Leonardo da Vinci's Battle of Anghiari in the Palazzo Vecchio in Florence. A fine posthumous satisfaction for this anonymous medieval artist.

Piazza della Scala and Porta Settimiana

Leaving the church, we leave the square where it meets Via della Paglia and, with a further diversions onto Vicolo del Piede, we reach a small square, Piazza de' Renzi. It is full of restaurants with their outdoor tables. We stop to listen to a story over a

Interior of the Ancient Pharmacy of Santa Maria della Scala, the oldest in Rome. Established in 1600, it was known as the Pharmacy of the Popes.

hundred years old. Indeed, in this square lived Romeo Ottaviani, known as *Er Più de Trastevere*, meaning 'the best of Trastevere', a virtual and honorary position that Romeo, a postman and bouncer, earned on a night in 1899 in Via Frattina, when, in order to defend a badly beaten prostitute, he knocked out with a punch the *Malandrinone* (literally, 'the big rogue'), a well-known exponent of the Roman underworld.

Leaving the square, we take Via del Cipresso, which leads us to Vicolo del Cinque. Turning first left and then right a little further on, we find ourselves on Via della Scala. The square of the same name is our objective. Once there, our attention is immediately caught by the *Antica Farmacia* (Ancient Pharmacy) *di Santa Maria della Scala*. It is the oldest pharmacy in Rome. It was established in 1600 and was originally called the *Spezieria* (Apothecary's shop). Its current name is due to the church and convent of Santa Maria della Scala, which stand next to it. It was on the second floor of the convent that the Discalced Carmelites produced and sold their spices and medicines in their spezieria. It was called The Pharmacy of the Popes, given the illustrious guests who frequented it. Today the old apothecary's shop is a historical site that can be visited thanks to a special opening, while the ground floor houses a modern pharmacy. The most famous of the ancient medicines, still preserved today in a marble container, is the *Teriaca*, known since Roman times and once believed to be the panacea for all ills.

Porta Settimiana
It was built by Septimius Severus on the site of the Horti Getae.

From the square we can see *Porta Settimiana* ahead. We go towards it. The gate was built by Septimius Severus on the Horti Getae, Gardens of Septimius Geta, who was his son and brother of Caracalla.

An alley in Trastevere by night. The name of the district stems from the Latin expression Trans Tiberim, 'Beyond the Tiber'. It was the first to be built on the right bank of the river.

The gate as it stands today is the result of the reconstruction ordered by Pope Alexander VI Borgia in 1498 and has Ghibelline battlements as its distinctive feature. Standing in front of it at the intersection with Via

Garibaldi, we are in exactly the same spot as Carlo Verdone in a celebrated scene from his film *Un Sacco Bello*, the one where the simpleton Leo first destroys a demijohn of oil and then meets the Spanish Marisol struggling to find the Youth Hostel. *Porta Settimiana* marks the beginning of Via della Lungara, on

Palazzo Corsini
It currently houses one of the two branches of the National Gallery of Ancient Art.

which we walk. Started under Alexander VI, it was definitively laid out under Julius II Della Rovere (1503-1511) who wanted it symmetrical to Via Giulia, which is on the other side of the Tiber. The appellation Lungara is due to the length of the straight stretch. About halfway along we stop to look at *Palazzo Corsini* on the left, currently one of the two sites of the Galleria Nazionale d'Arte Antica (National Gallery of Ancient Art). Its grand triple-arched portal with balcony above is remarkable. The Gallery is located on the main floor and is, of course, open to visitors. The palace was originally called Villa Riario and had a different layout to the one we see today. To the Corsinis, who renovated it, it was sold in 1736 by Duke Nicola Riario Sforza. How did the art collection come down to us?

Through the institution of the Fidecommissum, which was in force in Rome between the 17th and 18th centuries and forbade the sale of family-owned works of art. And so, when the Corsini family sold the entire palace to the Italian State in 1883, they also gifted us with their precious collection. When it was still called *Villa Riario*, Queen Christina of Sweden lived here. And in what

81

Botanical Garden of Rome. One of the largest in Italy, it is located on part of the archaeological area called Horti Getae.

is known as the *Sala dell'Alcova* ('Alcove Room') she died on 19 April 1683. A plaque bears her testamentary words:

"I was born free, I lived free and I shall die free".

The garden behind the palace once reached as far as the slopes of the Janiculum Hill. It is now largely incorporated by the Botanical Garden of Rome, itself open to visitors.

Opposite Palazzo Corsini stands a true Renaissance architectural gem: *Villa Farnesina*. It was built between 1505 and 1520 by Baldassarre Peruzzi on behalf of the banker Agostino Chigi, known as The Magnificent, the richest man in the world at the time. The palace was Agostino's wedding gift to his future wife Francesca Ordeaschi. Chigi was truly a character sui generis. A patron of the arts, although he could marry any noble woman he wanted, he decided to wed Ordeaschi, who not only was not a princess, but was rumoured to have been saved by the marriage from a future of prostitution. The wedding was celebrated by Pope Leo X himself. Not only that, every time Augustine organised a sumptuous banquet, at the end he had the silver plates used during the evening thrown into the Tiber, to the amazement of the diners. Of course, as soon as the diners stepped out of the palace along with their amazement, Augustine would order his servants to retrieve the silver plates through an ingenious system of nets he had devised and placed at the bottom of the river.

From an artistic point of view, the villa is full of masterpieces. Starting on the ground floor with the *Loggia di Galatea* (Galatea's Loggia), whose name is due to Raphael's fresco of the same name standing out on one of the long walls. On the upper floor

Loggia di Galatea and Villa Farnesina
The loggia is named after the fresco painted here by Raphael Sanzio.

Statue of the Roman poet Trilussa in the square of the same name. Born Carlo
Alberto Salustri, one of his most famous compositions is 'Ninna Nanna della
Guerra'('War's Lullaby'), composed in 1914.

is the evocative *Sala Delle Prospettive* (Hall of Perspectives), the work of Peruzzi, who frescoed the walls with both rural and urban perspective views between fake columns. When observing them, one truly has the impression that the room opens up to reveal a balcony and the landscape in the background. Approaching this fresco, we find a surprise: an inscription defaces the work right in the middle of the two columns. It bears the date 1527, when the Sack of Rome took place. It was the Lansquenets who engraved it and it reads in German:

"Why talk and not laugh if we scared the Pope away?".

Before leaving the building, a visit to Augustine and Francesca's bedroom is a must. The main fresco, covering the entire north wall, is the sensual *Nozze di Alessandro e Roxane* (The Marriage of Alexander and Roxane) by Sodom. The scene depicts Alexander handing the sceptre to a nude Roxane at the foot of the bed. All around is a riot of cupids. The most attractive of them is the one crouched at her feet.

Back on Via della Lungara, it is time to wrap up this itinerary of ours. We do so by reaching the nearby Piazza Trilussa, which is often cited as the epicentre of Rome's unruly nightlife. By day, however, it is a relatively quiet square. We stop in front of the statue of the poet, Belli's twentieth-century heir, where one of his poems is inscribed in stone: the title is 'In the shade'.

In the Shade

*Mentre me leggo er solito giornale
Spaparanzato all'ombra d'un pajaro
Vedo un porco e je dico: Addio Maiale!
Vedo un ciuccio e je dico: Addio Somaro!*

*Maybe these beasts won't understand me
But at least I feel the satisfaction
of being able to call a spade a spade
Without the fear of ending up in prison.*

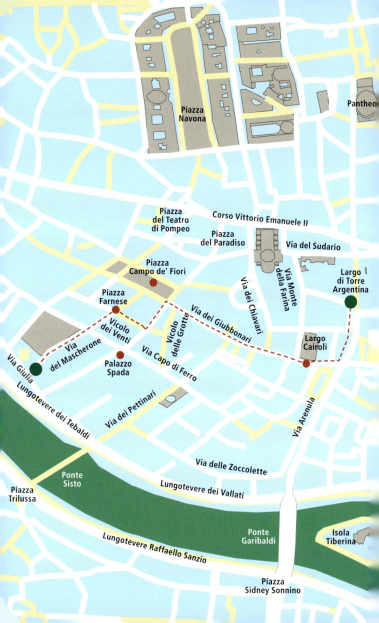

Around Campo de' Fiori

Via Giulia - Fontana del Mascherone

Our itinerary starts from Via Giulia, near *Fontana del Mascherone* ('Fountain of the Mask'). In medieval times the street was called *Magistralis*, because it was considered a main road. Under Sixtus IV it underwent its first restructuring and took the name *Via Mercatoria*, because it connected areas of high financial potential (Ponte Sant'Angelo with the Markets of Campo de' Fiori and Piazza Navona). In 1508 the ultimate turning point: Julius II commissioned Bramante to design the longest straight road in Rome: 1 km. He gave it his name. Such it still is today.

From our standpoint we can admire right above us the Arco Farnese, which in Michelangelo's original plans should have been the starting point of a bridge connecting Palazzo Farnese and Villa Farnesina, on the other side of the Tiber. This project remained unfinished and so today the Arch has the sole function of giving the street a more striking appearance. To our left is the *Fontana del Mascherone*, famous for the huge mask of ancient Roman origin depicting a head with its mouth open. The Farnese family wanted it to become a public drinking trough and - imagine that! - in 1720 for three days, in honour of the Grand Knight of Malta Zondari, it spouted wine. Presumably very merry days for the people of Rome.

At this point we begin our walk by turning right onto Via del Mascherone. About halfway down the street we find a plaque high up on our right, reminding us of the passage through the palace of a certain Waiblinger, an artist unknown to most, but who *"Departed from his native Germany and found the home of his dreams in this immortal Rome. Here only happy"*.

A glimpse of Via Giulia with the Farnese Arch in the foreground. Known as 'Magistralis' in medieval times, it is a straight stretch of 1 km and is dedicated to Pope Julius II, who commissioned it.

From the protagonist of a historical Grand Tour comes an implicit blessing to our Little Grand Tour.

Piazza Farnese

At the end of the street we come to Piazza Farnese. In the centre of it are two exquisite fountains, which were originally two granite basins from the Baths of Caracalla, and which were refurbished by Girolamo Rainaldi in 1626. The square got its name from the imposing palace that towers over it. It is one of the most beautiful Roman palaces and is called *the Dice* because of its compactness. It was commissioned by the future Pope Paul III when he was still a cardinal. He commissioned Sangallo who worked on it until his death in 1546. He was later succeeded by Michelangelo, who redefined the façade. The palace was later taken over by Vignola, who saw to the completion of the rear façade. The work was then completed by Della Porta in 1589. If we pause to admire the façade, we will be captivated by the cornice decorated with lilies surmounted by a frieze alternating lion heads with drops. Seat of the French embassy, it is not open to visitors, save for rare exceptions. In the rooms inside, apart from the ballroom, the *Farnese Gallery* deserves special mention, with frescoes painted in the late 16th century by Annibale Carracci. They are considered the Sistine Chapel of the Bolognese painter and for many scholars represent the forerunner of the Roman Baroque, especially for their use of perspective illusionism.

Fontana del Mascherone a Via Giulia
The Farnese family wanted it as a public trough.

One of the two fountains in Piazza Farnese. Placed here by Giacomo Rainal in 1626, they are two granite basins originally part of the Baths of Caracalla.

Palazzo Spada

At the intersection with Via del Mascherone we take Via de Venti and soon find ourselves in Piazza Capo di Ferro, facing Palazzo Spada. It is the seat of the Italian Council of State and houses the Borromini's famous Perspective Corridor. It is a small pyramid-shaped gallery that rises in a courtyard inside the palace. This gallery is apparently about forty metres deep and ends in a green space with a statue of a small warrior about one and a half metres tall. *'Apparently'* is precisely the right term to use in this case. In fact, we are in the presence of a masterful optical illusion devised by the Baroque genius of Borromini. One only has to enter the gallery to realise it. In reality, the Gallery measures 8.82 metres in length, the backdrop is painted with mock vegetation, and the Roman-era warrior statue measures a mere 80 centimetres in height. The illusion is given by the convergence of the planes of the colonnade, which, instead of proceeding parallel, converge towards a single vanishing point, degrading from top to bottom and shrinking at the bottom, while the mosaic floor rises. So much so that the first columns measure three metres in height while the last just 1.70 metres. Borromini completed this work in just one year, between 1652 and 1653, on behalf of Bernardino Spada, who was crazy about plays of perspective.

Borromini's perspective
It is located inside Palazzo Spada and is a masterpiece of optical illusion.

Piazza Campo de' Fiori on market mornings. The statue of Giordano Bruno, w
was burnt alive here in 1600, is clearly visible. The work by Ettore Ferrari, it
dated 1889.

Piazza Campo de' Fiori and statue of Giordano Bruno

Leaving the palace, it is time for us to reach the heart of this itinerary: *Campo de' Fiori*. It is just a five-minute walk. If we find ourselves in this square on a weekday morning, we will be enraptured by the atmosphere of its outdoor market. The name of the square is linked to its origins, when it was a simple meadow in bloom, used for cattle grazing, near the ruins of the *Theatre of Pompey*, the first permanent theatre built entirely in masonry. The square was paved by Eugene IV around 1440 and immediately became an important city hub with, in addition to the market, hotels, inns, bookshops and courtesans' houses. It also became known in history as the place of torture, in 1600, of the philosopher Giordano Bruno, who was burnt alive. There is a monument in the centre of the square to remind us of this. The statue, the work of Ettore Ferrari, was erected on 9 June 1889. For its creation, men of culture from all over Europe raised the necessary funds. Giordano Bruno is immortalised in a philosopher's pose, with his hands crossed over his closed book. The statue is made of bronze and was cast at the Crescenzi foundry in Rome.

Giordano Bruno
The philosopher was burnt alive in Campo de' Fiori in 1600.

To leave the square, we take Via dei Giubbonari, named after the artisans and merchants of *gipponi* (called *Gipponari*, i.e. bodice weavers). This street has a unique feature: it belongs to three districts. The left side, coming from Campo de' Fiori and up to the junction with Via dei Chiavari, belongs to *Rione Parione*; the remaining left side up to Piazza Cairoli belongs to *Rione Sant'Eustachio*, while the entire right side is part of *Rione Regola*.

Area Sacra di largo Argentina with the theatre in the background. The Area came to light in 1926 during the demolition of the church of San Nicola de' Cesarini

Largo di Torre Argentina

In Piazza Benedetto Cairoli, the church of San Carlo ai Catinari deserves our attention. The correct name is San Biagio and San Carlo ai Catinari. The appellation Catinari refers to the manufacturers of basins that used to be located at this spot in the Sant'Eustachio district. Once inside, we pause to look under the dome: in size it is the third largest in ancient Rome after those of St Peter's and Sant'Andrea della Valle.

Leaving the church, we take Via Arenula on our left. We soon find ourselves in Largo di Torre Argentina, the final stop on this itinerary. Facing us is the *Teatro Argentina*, the second oldest theatre in Rome after the *Teatro Valle*. It was inaugurated on 31 January 1732 with Domenico Sarro's *Berenice*. A date certainly worth remembering is also 20 February 1816, when the premiere of *The Barber of Seville* by Gioachino Rossini was held here. The premiere turned out to be a fiasco, fortunately recovered thanks to subsequent performances that established its everlasting success.

Opposite the theatre is the *Area Sacra of Largo Argentina*, which was discovered in 1926 during the demolition of the church of *San Nicola de' Cesarini*. Here the remains of four temples from the Republican era are preserved. According to several experts, the assassination of Julius Caesar during the famous Ides of March took place here. Nowadays, the place is home to a significant feline colony. Let us try peeking over the balustrade to catch a glimpse of some of the cats.

The cats of Torre Argentina
A real feline colony populates the archaeological area of Largo Argentina. The cats are cared for by the Associazione Culturale Colonia Felina di Torre Argentina.

95

Roman Ghetto

Piazza Mattei and Fontana delle Tartarughe

The *Serraglio degli Hebrei* (Jewish Seraglio) was established on 14 July 1555 by Pope Paul IV with the papal bull *Cum Nimis Absurdum*, complete with a three-door wall on Piazza Giudea, near Sant'Angelo in Pescheria and San Gregorio, in the Sant'Angelo district. In the beginning, 2000 people lived there. Thirty years later Sixtus V enlarged it by extending it towards the Tiber, so that the area took on the shape of a trapezium. The two longest sides measured 270 metres on the river and 180 on Via della Pescheria, while the depth between the Tiber and Via della Pescheria was 150 metres. It was closed from dusk to dawn, when the gates opened and only those with a permit could enter. The hygienic conditions were appalling, with frequent epidemics due to the lack of public fountains. Consider that, for a long time, the inhabitants had to drink river water. By the early 19th century the population of the *Ghetto* had risen to 8000. This is why Pope Leo XII decided in 1826 to enlarge the Ghetto by encompassing the strip up to Piazza Mattei.

And it is from this square that our itinerary begins. The place name is linked to the Mattei family, whose properties had developed into a built-up area. The oldest building is that of Giacomo Mattei, erected in the second half of the 15th century. The building at No. 19 is the oldest, the work of a disciple of Rossellino, and features a beautiful white marble portal with the family coat of arms and a courtyard with an elegant loggia. On the façade of No. 17, there is a walled-in window. According to a legend, it was walled up on the orders of one of the Mattei dukes, after his future father-in-law saw the *Fontana delle Tartarughe* ('Turtle Fountain'), which stands opposite the palace, built in one night in response to

Aerial view of part of the Ghetto, clearly showing Theatre of Marcellus and the Synagogue.

his doubts about the future groom's solvency following a loss at the gaming tables.

"That's what a penniless Mattei is capable of doing in a few hours!" the Duke is said to have shouted and, having had his bride-to-be's hand back, he had the window walled up.

The Turtle Fountain is the attraction of the square and was built between 1581 and 1584 by Taddeo Landini to a design by Giacomo della Porta. It features four bronze ephebes resting their feet on the same number of dolphins; the bronze turtles were added later by Gian Lorenzo Bernini.

Fontana delle Tartarughe
It was built between 1581 and 1584 by Taddeo Landini from a design by by Giacomo della Porta.

In the heart of the Ghetto

We leave the square by taking Via dei Funari until we turn right onto Piazza Lovatelli. Before us is the palace of the same name, built in 1580 by Gian Filippo Serlupi and later owned by the Lovatelli family. The square itself was once called Piazza Serlupi. It was here that Countess Ersilia Caetani Lovatelli, who was appointed academician of the Lincei, held open salons for artists and men of letters, including Carducci, Gregorovius, D'Annunzio, Zola and Liszt.

To get into the heart of the Ghetto, from Piazza Lovatelli we decide to take Via di Sant'Angelo in Pescheria, named after the church that the street runs alongside and whose side entrance faces it. The church dates back to 770 and was built by Theodore, uncle of Pope Hadrian I. It was so called because of the fish market that was held at the Portico d'Ottavia, *Forum Piscium* or *Foro Piscario*. Having fallen into ruin, it underwent rebuilding and finally restoration in 1610. In 1343, it was from here that Cola di Rienzo set out to conquer the Capitol, and it was here that, until the 18th century, the Jews were forced to attend church on

Portico d'Ottavia al Ghetto. The complex was rebuilt on the site of the ancie[nt] Portico of Metellus. It was commissioned by Augustus between 27 and 23 B[C] and dedicated to his sister Octavia.

Saturdays and hear the Jesuits preach to convert them. According to legend, the Jews would plug their ears in order not to hear the sermon. The scene was referenced by Luigi Magni in his famous film *The Conspirators*.

At the end of the street we cross an archway carved out of the ruins of the ancient *Portico d'Ottavia*: it is the street of the same name that welcomes us. We walk along it until we reach Largo 16 Ottobre. We admire what remains of the ancient complex from the Augustan age. It was rebuilt by the Emperor Augustus between 27 and 23 BC in place of the older *Portico of Metellus* and was dedicated to his beloved sister Octavia. Partially destroyed by fire in 191, it was rebuilt by Septimius Severus in 203. And it is precisely to this period that most of today's visible ruins belong.

The second thing we do is to turn our gaze to our right towards the plaque commemorating the infamous rounding up of the Ghetto by the Nazis on 16 October 1943. Of the more than a thousand rounded up and taken to Auschwitz on the sealed trains, only sixteen returned.

Tempio Maggiore

Taking Viale del Portico d'Ottavia, we come to the Great Synagogue, also known as the Tempio Maggiore. It dates back to 1904 and was built by architects Armanni and Costa on the site of the ancient place of worship, *Le Cinque Scole* (The Five Schools, or Synagogues). With a square base, the Synagogue is topped by a large alumin-

The Synagogue as seen from the edge of the Theatre of Marcellus. The latter originally a theatre in Ancient Rome, was occupied by small dwellings durir the Middle Ages.

ium dome. Divided into two sto-
reys, the first houses the temple
proper, with a central nave and
two small side aisles, at the end of
which are two small Arons from
the ancient Schools, while the
main Aron is located at the end
of the central nave. What is the
Aron? A sacred furnishing of the
Jewish religion, which holds the
Torah, the sacred scrolls.

**Bas-relief
in the Ghetto**
The 'Jewish
Seraglio' was
decreed on 14
July 1555 by Pope
Paul IV.

On the lower floor is the Jewish Museum. Speaking of the aforementioned Five Schools, there is a
square of the same name just beyond the Synagogue.
It is Piazza delle Cinque Scole, named after the
building that housed the five Jewish schools (Scola
Nova, Scola del Tempio, La Siciliana, La Catalana, La Castigli-
ana). Opposite the building is the *Fontana del Pianto* ('Fountain
of Tears') dating from the late 16th century and created by Giacomo della Porta. It originally stood outside the Church of Santa
Maria del Pianto in Piazza Giudea. It was erected by Gregory
XIII, *"so that the Jews too might have refreshment from the water and
beautification".* It was placed in this square in 1970. At the time
of the historic Ghetto, it was located near the pole where *Justitia
per gli Hebrei* was done, i.e. where crimes committed by Jews were
judged and where *"The pawns that the Jews hold"* were auctioned.

To conclude our walk, it is fair to ask: when did the Jewish
segregation of the Ghetto end? It took the Unification of Italy
and the end of the temporal power of the popes. From then on,
Jews were put on an equal footing with other Italian citizens, as
was only right.

Capitol and Colosseum

An unusual view over Rome

Our itinerary begins at the splendid *Terrazza Caffarelli*, which houses the cafeteria bar of the Capitoline Museums below. It is one of the most striking and lesser-known views of Rome's rooftops and domes.

Once back on the street, Michelangelo's *Piazza del Campidoglio* awaits us on our right. It was designed in the shape of a trapezium, with the three Capitoline palaces occupying the three sides and appearing to protect the equestrian statue of Marcus Aurelius.

The staircase sloping gently up towards the square is also by Michelangelo and is known as *Cordonata del Campidoglio*.

The statue of Marcus Aurelius on horseback is actually a copy whose original we will soon admire in the Capitoline Museums.

The *Capitoline Museums* hold the city's oldest public art collection. Its origin dates back to 1471, when Sixtus IV donated the Lateran bronze collection to the city. Among the first rooms to be admired is the *Sala degli Orazi e dei Curiazi*. The fresco of the same name that unfolds before our eyes is by Cavalier D'Arpino (Giuseppe Cesari), a leading exponent of Roman Mannerism. He also worked on the other frescoes in this room. Commissioned in 1595, he was supposed to finish in 1600, the Jubilee year. In truth, he had only finished three scenes in 1613 and, after an interruption of twenty years, completed the work in 1640. A delay that was compensated for by the excellent quality of the work. In addition to the frescoes by Cavalier D'Arpino, this room is graced by the honorary statue of Urban VIII by Gian Lorenzo Bernini (1635-1640). Another compulsory stop is in the Hall of the Cap-

Capitol Square. Designed in the shape of a trapezoid by Michelangelo, it house
at its centre a copy of the statue of Marcus Aurelius, the original of which is insid
the Capitoline Museums.

itoline She-wolf, so called because of the masterpiece of ancient bronze sculpture (5th century BC), which is the very symbol of the city and has come down to us overcoming any impediment, from neglect to barbarian invasions, passing through a lightning strike that in 65 BC crushed its two twins below. The She-wolf arrived in the Capitol in 1471, donated by Sixtus IV, who added the sum of ten florins for the reconstruction of the twins. He was satisfied, probably thanks to the casting work of Antonio Pollaiolo. The statue was originally placed on the façade of the *Palazzo dei Conservatori*, then moved here at the end of the 16th century. The cult site of this wing of the Capitoline Museums is certainly the *Esedra del Marco Aurelio*, where the original statue of the emperor shines. He died in 180, exhausted by the exertions of war and a violent plague while in the camp of Vindobona (Vienna) during one of his countless campaigns. Linked to his death or the celebration of his victory over the Germanic peoples (176) was the decision to erect the equestrian statue of him that we have before us. Equestrian statues were very numerous in Rome at that time. Late imperial descriptions of the city enumerated as many as 22 of them, calling them *Equi Magni*, i.e. greater than life. This of Marcus Aurelius has the merit of being the only one that has come down to us. At first it was probably in the Roman Forum, from where it was moved to the Lateran around the 8th century. Until the end of the 15th century it was nicknamed *Caballus Costantini*, because it was mistakenly thought to depict the first Christian emperor.

Capitoline She-wolf
A symbol of the city, it is a masterpiece of ancient bronze work (5th century BC).

In January 1538, by order of Pope Paul III and the Farnese family, the statue was moved to the Capitoline Hill. Within a year of its arrival, the Senate commissioned Michelangelo to arrange the

Remains of the colossal statue of Constantine. Located in Palazzo dei Conservatori, it was one of the main works of late antique Roman sculpture.

statue and he made it the pivot of the entire square. The statue was removed from Piazza del Campidoglio on 17 January 1981 for restoration, which was completed in 1988. It was placed here on 11 April 1990, in an air-conditioned, glass-enclosed chamber.

The Pinacoteca Capitolina, on the other hand, collects Italian paintings from the Middle Ages to the 18th century. It originate in the 18th century with the purchases of the Sacchetti (1748) and Pio di Savoia (1750) collections under Benedict XIV. The architect of the entire endeavour was Cardinal Silvio Valenti Gonzaga.

Leaving the Pinacoteca, we walk down the grand staircase until we reach the underground level where a connecting gallery, full of inscriptions, funerary and otherwise, leads us to the striking view of the *Tabularium*, once the seat of the Roman archives, a trapezoidal building with a strong indentation due to the presence of the ancient Temple of Veiove. We are exactly under the Palazzo Senatorio and the view of the expanse of the Roman Forum is highly suggestive: at our feet are the Arch of Septimius Severus, Via Sacra, to the left the Curia, then the ruins of the *Temple of Saturn*.

Once at *Palazzo Nuovo*, the last stop on our museum tour must be the Sala del Galata ('Hall of the Galatian'), named after the famous statue of the *Galata Morente* ('Dying Galatian'), found in 1622 in the Horti Sallustiani. It is an excellent replica of one of the sculptures that made up the monument that Attalus I (241-197 B.C.) had dedicated to Athena Pallas to mark his victories over the Galatians. The warrior is naked, fallen on his shield, his beautiful mournful head reclining in a last moment of resistance against death. His belonging to the Celtic peoples is emphasized by the presence

Dying Galatian
The statue was found in 1622 in the Horti Sallustiani. It is located in the Capitoline Museums.

The Roman Forum as seen from above. In the Middle Ages, the abandoned Forum became pasture land and was named Campo Vaccino.

of the Torques around his neck and the distinctive style of his mustache and hair.

Roman Forum

Leaving the museums, we descend the Capitoline cordonade. Walking to our right we find, after a few hundred meters, the Vittoriano, named after Victor Emmanuel II. It was designed by Sacconi and the foundation stone was laid in 1885. The inauguration, however, took place 26 years later, on June 4, 1911 to be exact, to coincide with the fiftieth anniversary of the Unification of Italy. The body of an unknown soldier who died during the Great War was buried here on August 4, 1921, and so from then on the building also began to be called the Altar of the Fatherland. It is 81 meters high, including the quadrigas at the top, and 135 meters wide. The gleaming white of the building is due to the Botticino marble used in its construction. The view of Rome enjoyed from the terrace at the top is 360 degrees and therefore exceptional. It is certainly worth a visit, made possible by a panoramic elevator.

Once back down and out, we take a right heading to the beginning of Via dei Fori Imperiali. Immediately, directly across from us, the Trajan's Column stands out within the Forum with the same name. It rises to a height of 29.77 meters, which become nearly 40 with the plinth and capital, and comprises 18 large, overlapping drums. Running in a spiral around the shaft is a frieze in relief composed of 2,500 figures. It depicts the defining moments of the two campaigns Trajan led against the Dacians, in 101-102 and 105-106 respectively.

Monument to Victor Emmanuel II Designed by Sacconi, it is 81 m high and 135 m wide.

Past the Column, a little further on we turn right onto Via di San Pietro in Carcere and quickly find ourselves

Trajan Column. Erected between 110 and 113 AD, it was a first in ancient art and became the most cutting-edge achievement for historical Roman relief.

on the esplanade of the Roman Forum. There is an admission fee to pay at the entrance, but for the cost of a single ticket you can also visit the Colosseum and the Palatine. The Roman Forum has a very ancient origin, but it did not take on its final appearance until the second century BC. At the time of the Republic it served both a social and political function. The latter function declined with the advent of the Imperial Age. With the collapse of the Western Roman Empire the Forum suffered the sad fate of many other glorious Roman landmarks: it was abandoned to gradual decay. During the Middle Ages it was a grazing land known as Campo Vaccino ('Cow Field'). It was only in the 19th century, thanks to the newfound Neoclassical sensibility, that archaeological excavations could begin and, despite a thousand impediments, succeed in bringing the Forum to light. Before our eyes today stands a long expanse of ruins. The main street is the famous *Via Sacra*, so called because at the time it stretched through sacred buildings and housed religious processions headed to the ancient *Temple of Jupiter Optimus Maximus* (or *Jupiter Capitolinus*). Immediately our attention is caught by the *Arch of Septimius Severus*. Standing 21 meters high and measuring 23 meters in width, it was erected in 203 AD in celebration of the Emperor, his two sons Caracalla and Geta and their victory over the Parthians.

Shortly thereafter we stop again at the *Curia Iulia* and *Lapis Niger*. The *Curia Iulia*, the seat of the Roman Senate, unlike the other buildings in the *Forum*, has survived through the centuries while retaining its original external appearance. It was Julius Caesar himself who wanted it here, while its current aspect is the result of a restoration ordered by

Arch of Septimius Severus
Built in 203 AD as a tribute to the Emperor and his two sons, Caracalla and Geta.

Detail of the bas-relief of the Arch of Titus. Roman soldiers parade with the spoils of the Temple of Jerusalem after its destruction in 71 AD.

Diocletian, following a fire that damaged it in 238 AD. The preservation of the Curia's architectural structure is due to the fact that in the 7th century AD the entire building was adapted into a church consecrated to St. Hadrian. This transformation ensured its inviolability. The *Lapis Niger*, black marble in a small square enclosure near the *Curia*, is a ruin that reaches us directly from the titanic era of the Seven Kings of Rome. In fact, it represents the place where Romulus was killed by the senators because of his despotic exercise of power. It is datable to the sixth century BC.

Past the *Lapis Niger*, we come to the *Basilica Aemilia*, whose present-day scattered vestiges make it difficult for us to imagine its ancient magnificence. It was built in 173 BC at the behest of the censors Marcus Aemilius Lepidus and Marcus Fulvius Nobiliorus. During the fifteenth century it was damaged by fire due to the infamous and disastrous Sack of Rome by Aldaric's Goths. There is still a trace of that barbaric act among the ruins of the Basilica, in the midst of which the coins that became molten on the occasion are still recognizable. Beyond the Basilica we find the remains of the *Temple of Caesar*, erected on the site of Julius Caesar's cremation after his assassination the Ides of March. Before the Temple was inaugurated on 18 August 29 BC at the behest of Augustus, a marble column with the inscription 'Parenti Patriae: to the Father of the Fatherland', stood on this same site. It is thought that the temple had been Corinthian and that the appellation Divus Julius was due to the fact that Julius Caesar had been deified, the first case of post-mortem divination. A curiosity: even today it happens to see tourists laying flowers near the temple ruins as a sign of respect for the immortal Roman leader.

Arch of Titus
According to tradition, the Jews never walked under it so as not to pay homage to those who destroyed their temple.

View of the interior of the Colosseum from above. Started by Vespasian and completed by his son Titus it was inaugurated on 21 April in the year 80 AD.

Colosseum

We leave the Fori behind passing under the *Arch of Titus*. The latter, completed in 81, was erected to commemorate the victory of Vespasian and Titus over the Jews and the taking of Jerusalem in 79. Titus died the same year as its completion and so the task of its inauguration fell to his successor Domitian. Here are its dimensions: 15.40 meters high, 13.50 meters wide and one archway. Tradition tells us that the Jews never passed under it so as not to pay homage to those who had destroyed their temple.

Speaking of ancient Rome's arches, we are about to approach the most famous one: the *Arch of Constantine*. It was erected to celebrate the latter's victory over Maxentius at the Battle of the Milvian Bridge (October 28, 312). It was dedicated to him on July 25, 315, and is an authentic hymn to the recycling of luxury. Indeed, the Corinthian columns were parts of a Domitian monument, the two reliefs inside the archway derive from the Trajan Forum, the statues of captive barbarians on the top are from Hadrian's time, and the eight reliefs next to the inscriptions belonged to an Arch of Marcus Aurelius.

Beyond the Arch of Constantine we catch a glimpse of the unmistakable silhouette of the *Colosseum*. The real name of the monument is *Flavian Amphitheater*, for it was the Flavian family that wanted it built. Vespasian began it and his son Titus completed the work, inaugurating it on 21 April 80 AD. Why is it called the Colosseum? There are four possible explanations. The first: the name comes from the appellation of an ancient statue of Nero, called The Colossus, which stood near-by. The second: the name comes from the location of the monument, formerly Collis Isei, on account of a Temple of Isis. The third: the name comes simply

External view of the Colosseum
It has a girth of 527 meters and a height of 57.

The Arch of Constantine as seen from an opening in the Colosseum. The Arc was erected in celebration of the emperor's victory over Maxentius at the Battle Ponte Milvio (28 October 312).

from the imposing bulk of the building itself. With the fourth explanation we definitely enters the world of legend. Accordingly, there was a time when the *Flavian Amphitheater* was a kind of devilish temple in which sor-

cerers asked followers Colis Eum? i.e., Do you worship Him? The He was obviously the Devil himself. It was a short step from Colis Eum to Colosseum.

The Flavian Amphitheater is large in scale: the axes of the ellipses measure 185 and 156 meters, the circumference is 527 meters, and the height totals 57 meters. To build it required 100,000 cubic meters of travertine and 300 tons of metal for the pivots to attach the blocks. The audience could reach 70,000, with access through 80 entrances. It was a prime site for gladiatorial encounters, venationes (hunting ferocious animals) and naumachiae (staging of naval battles). The advent of Christianization and the cessation of activity around the 6th century meant that over the next centuries the arena fell into disgrace, drowning in gradual, relentless decay. In the Middle Ages it even became the inhospitable home of murderers, thieves and prostitutes. Sixtus V was on the verge of having it demolished. Fortunately, he eventually changed his mind, opting for a starkly opposite choice: he included it in the itinerary of the basilicas. For the Colosseum it was the beginning of a rebirth, so much so that nowadays it is included in the list of the new 7 wonders of the world.

Monti

In the ancient Suburra

The first of Rome's districts is significantly large and includes, among other things, the two great basilicas of *Santa Maria Maggiore* and *San Giovanni in Laterano*. In our itinerary we decide to prioritize a portion of it, starting our walk from Piazza della Suburra, at the entrance to the Cavour metro station.

The name of this square is no accident. In Roman times the site constituted the heart of the Suburra, the city's working-class neighbourhood. Sub Urbe, that is, below the city proper, identified at the time with the Palatine. The Suburra was a residential neighbourhood with a very high housing concentration, very noisy and very hot in summer. In the collective imagination it was the site of prostitution and lechery par excellence. As a matter of fact, it also housed shops and workshops of everyday tradesmen, such as shoemakers, barbers, butchers, and innkeepers. With the fall of the Roman Empire, the district gradually transformed and was incorporated into the *Monti* district. During the Middle Ages it was by far the most prestigious in the city. To be clear, the head of the rione held the position of Prior, a role that guaranteed him participation in the government of the city. Not only that, the Montici dialect was noticeably different from those of the other wards.

With this in mind, don't you feel the urge to delve into the maze of its streets and distinctive views?

I believe you do. From Piazza della Suburra we decide to take Via Urbana, which corresponds to the ancient *Vicus Patricius*. Its current name is due to major extension and renovation works commissioned by Pope Urban VIII in the 17th century. A few

Scalinata dei Borgia (Staircase of the Borgias), also known as Vicus Scelerat A highly evocative sight, it connects Via Cavour with Piazza di San Pietro Vincoli above.

meters ahead we turn to our left to reach Piazza degli Zingari (Gypsy Square), so called because from the 17th century this site saw a high concentration of gypsies, who flocked here in caravans. Men worked metal pots and dishes, while women read the future into people's hands in exchange for donations. From the square we take Via dei Capocci. The latter was a noble family originally from Viterbo that died out in the male line in the mid-17th century. The street, which on its sides opens up the view to very picturesque alleys, leads us onto one of the most famous streets in the district: Via Panisperna. As we reach it and turn our gaze to our right, we feel the irresistible call of the *Basilica of Santa Maria Maggiore* towering in the background. We reach it after a series of ups and downs of the street. The origin of the Basilica is legendary: on the night between 4 and 5 August 356, the Virgin Mary came in a dream to a patrician named John and his wife, who, being childless, wished to dedicate a church to the Virgin. In the dream they were told that a miracle would reveal the place where the new church should be built. That same night Pope Liberius also had the same dream, and so the next day, having arrived at the Esquiline and found it miraculously whitened with snow, he himself drew the perimeter of the church, built, of course, at the expense of the patrician John. In short, everybody was happy. The designated name for the church was Santa Maria della Neve (St. Mary of the Snow). Even today, every 5th of August, the Miracle of the Snow is re-enacted through a cascade of white petals.

Moses by Michelangelo According to legend, once the work was completed, the artist struck its knee with the hammer, asking: "Why won't you speak?".

Altar of the Confession inside Basilica di Santa Maria Maggiore. Recognizab[le] from behind is the 19th-century statue of a praying Pius IX.

Santa Maria Maggiore

In contrast, the *Basilica of Santa Maria Maggiore*, which stands on the same miraculous site, was erected between 432 and 444 at the behest of Sixtus III, after the Council of Ephesus had sanctioned the dogma of the Divine Maternity. Let us head inside.

In the entrance portico we are awed, on the left, by the *Porta Santa* ('Holy Door'), and on the right by the *bronze statue of Philip IV of Spain*, a 1665 work by Bernini. The king had granted a rich bequest to the Basilica, and this was how the Liberian canons, who administered *Santa Maria Maggiore*, decided to repay themselves. Once inside, we can admire above our heads a beautiful coffered ceiling, a 15th-century work by Giuliano da Sangallo. We walk down the right aisle until we reach the Cappella Sistina. Compared to the more famous one, painted by Michelangelo and commissioned by Sixtus IV, this one was erected at the behest of Sixtus V, the urbanist Pope, who chose the site as the burial place of both himself and his patron Pius V. Just beyond the chapel we find the *Tomb of Gian Lorenzo Bernini*. What strikes us about this tomb is its simplicity, especially when compared with the magnificence of Bernini's work.

We make one last stop in this basilica by entering the *Cappella Paolina*, which is located in the left aisle. It was commissioned by Paul V Borghese and houses a painting on a wooden panel, in which the Blessed Virgin Mary, Mother of Jesus, is depicted holding a blessing baby Jesus. For many, this work dates back to the Liberian period of *Santa Maria della Neve* and has always been venerated as *Salus Populi Romani*, so much so that it is often carried out in procession through the streets of Rome.

Basilica of Santa Maria Maggiore
Outside this church, every August 5, the miracle of summer snowfall is celebrated. Not to be missed.

Glimpse of Via Panisperna with the Basilica of Santa Maria Maggiore clearly visible in the background.

Via Panisperna and Torre delle Milizie

Having received the Our Lady's blessing, we leave and restart our itinerary by turning onto Via Panisperna. We ask ourselves a question: why is it called like this?

There are many interpretations. The most reliable one refers to a papal bull of John XXII which mentioned the church of *San Lorenzo Parasperna*, a mix of the Greek word Para (Near) and the Old Latin word Sperno (Boundary) that was to indicate that the church was located on the border between major neighbouring properties. In any case, just at the corner with Via Milano, there is the very ancient church of *San Lorenzo in Panisperna*, which was built on the very site of the Saint's martyrdom. In walking down the street we find it on our right.

Not only art, though. The street is also linked to what colloquially came to be known as the 'boys of Via Panisperna' who were actually a group of Italian physicists headed by Enrico Fermi, who in the 1930s worked at the Royal Institute of Physics at the University of Rome, then located here at number 90. As we continue to walk on this street, also beloved by the great film director Mario Monicelli, who lived the last years of his life in the district, we begin to catch a glimpse of the bulk of the Torre delle Milizie on the horizon.

Before approaching it we find on our left, on largo Angelicum, the *Church of Santi Domenico e Sisto*, recognizable by its wide and distinctive double-flight staircase ending in an elliptical terrace.

As for *Torre delle Milizie*, which is now two stories as opposed to the original three, popular tradition tells us that it was from here that Nero contemplated the Great Fire of Rome while play-

Church of Saints Dominic and Sixtus
A beautiful view of the Militia Tower can be enjoyed from the elliptical terrace right at the top of the church's distinctive staircase.

Torre delle Milizie, a 13th-century fortress. The origin of its name is unknow

ing his notorious zither. It is actually a 13th-century fortress, and the origin of its name is unclear. During the 14th century the Annibaldi and Caetani families fought over it. This meant that, at that time, the leading Roman families liked to entrench themselves in real forts to defend themselves from the "outside." If we observe it carefully, it appears to be sloping. It is indeed so, and the cause was an the earthquake in 1348 which left a deep scar on it. At this point it is time for us to go downhill on the Salita del Grillo. The next stop takes place a hundred meters further down, at Palazzo del Grillo with its 13th-century tower. The palace was acquired by the Grillo family, originally from Gubbio, during the 17th century. Impossible not to immediately think of the great Alberto Sordi and his portrayal of the Marchese del Grillo.

Whereupon the question arises: Who was he?

No doubt a legendary character. A pamphlet preserved in the Capitoline archives tells us of a man renowned *"for the extravagant fashions of his clothes, for the mordacity of his witticisms, and for the vulgarity of the pranks he proposed and often delivered."* Some identify him as a certain Bernardino, an unrepentant bachelor who died around 1750. What is certain is that at the receiving end of his pranks were to be counted mainly Jews, to whom he often reserved downright cruel surprises.

Torre de' Conti
With its 29 m in height, it retains little of its original appearance due to the damage cause by the 1348 earthquake.

Toward Piazza della Madonna de' Monti

As we continue downhill we find on our right the *Arco dei Pantani* ('Arch of the Swamps'), which in Roman times provided the most traveled route between the Forums and the Suburra. It is currently used as a belvedere over the Forums of Augustus and Nerva. Why the designation? Because of

Night view of the Augustan Forum with Arco dei Pantani in the background. T arch, at 13-14 meters above sea level, is among the lowest places in the entire ci

the prolonged flooding the area suffered during the Middle Ages. After all, with its altitude - so to speak! - of 13-14 meters above sea level it is, along with the *Bocca della Verità* and *Piazza della Rotonda*, among the lowest sites in the entire city.

At the end of this descent, which meanwhile has turned into *Via Tor de' Conti*, we find the tower of the same name, the final one to be admired on this walk. It was erected by Lotario dei Conti in the 12th century and, like *Torre delle Milizie*, suffered huge damage during the 1348 earthquake. It currently measures 29 meters in height, nothing compared to its original size. Only the mighty bulk remains as a reminder of past splendour.

Having admired the tower, we briefly retrace our steps until we turn onto Via Baccina, which, with its tranquility and a plaque commemorating one of Ettore Petrolini's Roman residences, leads us to the final stop on our walk, namely Piazza della Madonna de' Monti. Lately the square has become a negative symbol of the Roman summer nightlife. And that's a pity, because although the nights are dominated by noise, during the day one can peacefully admire the beautiful fountain commissioned by Pope Sixtus V to Giacomo della Porta in 1588 and executed by the stonemason Battista Rusconi.

"Colonnacce". The only two columns left from the Forum of Nerva's colonnade.

Note that the coats of arms of Sixtus V and those of the Roman people alternate on the basin, proof that the civic administration of the time made its valuable contribution.

A gift we still blissfully enjoy today.

Beyond the Quirinale

On Rome's highest hill

To the delight of lovers of the film La Dolce Vita, Piazza di Trevi and its celebrated fountain serve as the starting point of our new itinerary.

The fountain spans the entire minor flank of Palazzo Poli: it is 20 m wide, and 26 m high, and is fronted by a triumphal arch formed by two orders of four columns topped by an attic. In the middle stands the statue of Oceanus on a shell-shaped chariot, drawn by two sea horses driven by two tritons.

The statue is the work of Pietro Bacci, while the construction of the fountain required the work of two architects. It was Nicola Salvi who began the work in 1733, under the pontificate of Clement XII. It was then completed in 1762 by Giuseppe Pannini, under Clement XIII.

Having closed our eyes and tossed the coin behind us into the fountain, we leave the square heading for the Quirinale. We get there by climbing Via della Dataria. Having reached the square in front of the palace, from this point on, the rest of our route will be straight up to *Porta Pia*.

We are in the highest of the seven Roman hills of legend. By the mid-sixteenth century, it was taken to be called *Monte Cavallo*. Our first glance goes to the imposing *Fontana dei Dioscuri*, in the centre of which stand the statues of the colossi Castor and Pollux flanked by their respective horses. These two statues had come to light in the ruins of the Baths of Constantine. Until 1589, the two statues flanked an old fountain and faced today's Palazzo della Consulta. It was Sixtus V who wanted to move Castor and Pollux further back and build the palace, now

Fontana dei Dioscuri with the Quirinale in the background. The obelisk is fro.
Campo Marzio, while the drinking fountain is from the Roman Forum.

known as *Palazzo Quirinale*, in front of it. At the turn of the 18th century and the beginning of the following century, the fountain took on its present appearance: first, an obelisk from *Campo Marzio* was erected between the two Dioscuri, and then a large watering trough taken from the *Roman Forum* was placed on site. Having let our gaze wander from the fountain to the beautiful panorama in the background, in which St. Peter's dome stands out in the distance, let us now focus on *Palazzo del Quirinale*. Gregory XIII wanted it as a summer residence. Its first architect in 1574 was Flaminio Ponzio, to whom we owe the grand staircase and who was followed by Mascherino. The latter was responsible for the large courtyard and the small palace, which was completed in 1582. The left side, toward Via della Dataria, was later built by Domenico Fontana at the behest of Sixtus V, who was the first Pope to die within these walls. The so-called *Manica Lunga* (Long Sleeve, i.e. Long Wing), which runs along Via Venti Settembre, is an even later work by Maderno. The palace has been a Papal residence since the late 16th century. During the 19th century, it hosted as many as four conclaves, with the Cappella Paolina used for polling and the *Manica Lunga* serving as the Cardinals' residence.

Statue of a Dioscurus
The two statues of Castor and Pollux, which grace the fountain in front of Palazzo Quirinale, come from the ruins of the Baths of Constantine

During the Roman Republic of 1849 it was occupied by the triumvirates of the Republic and so, when this experience was over, Pius IX, returning from exile in Gaeta, no longer wanted to live here and moved to the Vatican. After the breach of Porta Pia in 1870, the Kings of Italy took possession of the property by holding the famous Wednesday dance parties, alternating with the social-literary Thursday gatherings attended by the most fashionable members of Roman

The dome of San Carlo alle Quattro Fontane seen from the inside. A work of Borromini and a masterpiece of very small dimensions, it covers the area of only one of the four pillars that support St. Peter's Dome.

culture. Since 1947 it has been the seat of the Presidency of the Italian Republic.

Leaving the square and having begun to walk along Via Venti Settembre, on our right we find the *Gardens of Palazzo Quirinale*, at the heart of which stands the equestrian monument to Carlo Alberto, the work of Raffaello Romanelli erected in 1900. Staying on the street side of the garden, a little further on we find the church of *Sant'Andrea del Quirinale*, of the Jesuit fathers. Considered the pearl of the Baroque, it is the work of Gian Lorenzo Bernini and was built between 1658 and 1670. Once inside, we admire the polychrome marbles, gilding, and stucco decorating an oval structure, whose major axis is transverse and leads our gaze to the apse where stands the Borgognone altarpiece depicting *The Martyrdom of St. Andrew*.

A few hundred meters beyond this church we come across the genius of Bernini's arch-rival, namely Borromini. We do so by stopping to stare at the façade of *San Carlino alle Quattro Fontane*, a church that the architect erected between 1638 and 1641 and was completed after his death, probably by his nephew Bernardo. The diminutive Carlino is due to its small size. Think of it covering the area of only one of the four pillars supporting the dome of St. Peter's. In stark contrast to *Sant'Andrea al Quirinale*, the interior is austere, with the ellipsoidal space entirely dominated by a near-white colour. If one stares at the dome and its lantern, one has a strong urge to ascend, an aim that the very religious Borromini certainly did not despise. In conclusion to the visit, we move to the small cloister at the end of the right aisle: it has two floors and a small well in the centre, again by Borromini.

St. Andrew's on the Quirinal
Built by Bernini between 1658-1670, it is considered the pearl of the Baroque.

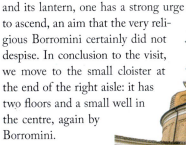

The statue of Moses by Leonardo Sormani. It was despised by the Romans, who called it 'the Ridiculous Moses'.

Beyond Via delle Quattro Fontane

Back on Via Venti Settembre, we pass the intersection with Via delle Quattro Fontane and continue our straight path. Having reached Largo di Santa Susanna, in front of us we find the *Fontana del Mosè*, also known as the Fontana dell'Acqua Felice ('Happy Water Fountain'). Made by Domenico Fontana, it was inaugurated in 1589. It is all travertine, arranged in three large niches punctuated by four columns in symmetry with four Egyptian lions placed on the basins. In the central niche is the massive statue of Moses, the work of Leonardo Sormani. The Romans did not much appreciate this statue and called it the *Mosè Ridicolo* ('Ridiculous Moses').

To the left of the fountain we find the *Church of Santa Maria della Vittoria*. Here Bernini's theatrical and Baroque taste was pushed to its zenith. The name of the church is due to an image of the Virgin Mary that was found in the garbage of Pilsen Castle and was credited with the victory, in 1620, of Ferdinand II of Habsburg over Protestant Prague. Before entering we learn another curiosity: also in those years of construction, digging in the foundations, the Hermaphrodite was found, a splendid Roman sculpture that can still be admired today in the Galleria Borghese. Once inside, we head to the left transept where Bernini's coup de théâtre awaits us: the *Ecstasy of Saint Theresa*.

Fontana del Tevere
Part of the Four Fountains complex, which gives its name to the street that runs through it.

"I saw near me, on my left side, an angel in bodily form...that cherub held in his hand a long golden dart...he seemed to thrust it repeatedly into my heart...when I was in this state I went as if out of my

Ecstasy of Saint Theresa by Gian Lorenzo Bernini. It is located inside Santa Maria della Vittoria and is considered one of his best works.

mind. I did not want to see or speak to anyone, but to be alone with my torment which seemed to me the greatest joy of any in creation...."

These are some of the words with which the Saint described her ecstasy and this is the event that Bernini carved in stone. For the sculptor from Campania it was one of his best works. In looking at it we can hardly believe it, fascinated and disturbed by the extraordinary sensuality with which it is cloaked. The dominant aspect is the light with which the saint is illuminated, descending from a special hidden lantern.

On seeing her, the Marquis De Sade sentenced, *"One can hardly believe that she is a saint."* While Charles de Brosses ironically remarked, *"If this is divine love, I know it well!"*

Leaving the church, we turn to our left heading for the last stop on this itinerary: *Porta Pia*. The Porta is in the Aurelian walls and was built by Michelangelo between 1561 and 1564, at the behest of Pius IV. It came to replace the ancient *Porta Nomentana*, which had lost its functionality. Also by Michelangelo is the interior façade decoration showing a motif of patens encircled by a stole. In the centre of these patens is a marble cube. In seeing them one gets the impression that they are patens with a towel around them and a piece of soap in the centre. According to popular belief, we are in the presence of a joke that Michelangelo wanted to play on Pius IV Medici, who did not belong to the famous Florentine family, but was said to be descended from Milanese barbers. During the cannonade of September 20, 1870, the breach was opened a short distance from the Porta. The latter thus suffered some damage. Nowadays the premises inside it house the *Historical Museum of the Bersaglieri* with its memorabilia.

Porta Pia
It was built by Michelangelo between 1561 and 1564. The Florentine genius also decorated its interior façade.

Villa Paganini

Via Nomentana

Corso Trieste

Via Alessandro Torlonia

Casino Nobile

Casina
delle Civette

Bunker
di Mussolini

Teatro di
Villa Torlonia

Via Lazzaro Spallanzani

Via Celso

Via Siracusa

Viale Regina Margherita

Via Antonio Musa

Via Bari

Via Morgagni

Viale del Policlinico

M Policlinico

Viale
Regina Elena

Villa Torlonia

A corner of paradise in the heart of Rome

Just beyond Porta Pia, along Via Nomentana, is the beautiful park of Villa Torlonia, in the Romantic style with ruins and exotic vegetation. It is worth our visit. It is the most recent of Rome's noble villas. It was originally an agricultural property of the Pamphilj family, which in the late 1700s Giovanni Torlonia bought and elected as his residence. During the same period, *Casino Nobile* and *Casino dei Principi* were built. During the 19th century, there were more extensions. After that followed years of neglect, which ended in the 1920s when this place became the residence of the Mussolini family. The latter inhabited Casino Nobile, which is the first mandatory stop on a walk inside the villa. Now a museum venue, built in full Neoclassical style, during restoration works, it unveiled a labyrinthine Etruscan tomb, from which departed a circuit of bunkers and air-raid shelter cellars dating back to World War II. The Casino was built between 1832 and 1840 under the direction of G.B. Caretti. Its interior can be accessed by walking down a grand staircase. Inside are 12 rooms and a ballroom decorated with a collection of Futurist paintings.

Aside from *Casino Nobile* one of the main attractions of the villa is certainly Casina delle Civette. As soon as you reach its presence you enter a fairy-tale dimension. The current building is the result of several transformations that have taken place since the 19th century. Founded as the *Capanna Svizzera* (Swiss Hut) in 1840 at the behest of Prince Alessandro Torlonia and the work of Giuseppe Jappelli, it

The park of Villa Torlonia with its distinctive palm trees and Egyptian obelisk
The villa is the most recent of Rome's aristocratic villas.

was initially a rustic artifact with the exteriors made of tuff ashlars and the interior painted in tempera in imitation of a classic Alpine hut. It was Alessandro Torlonia's grandson, Giovanni, who in the early 1900s wanted to change the appearance of this building. He commissioned architect Enrico Gennari, who created windows, loggias, porticos, turrets, majolica decorations and stained glass windows. And it was one of these stained glass windows that would cause the structure to change its name. In fact, in 1914 a stained-glass window designed by Duilio Cambellotti was installed, depicting two owls and ivy shoots. Hence the name *Casina delle Civette* (House of the Owls). The choice of owls was not accidental and had esoteric motivation. In fact, in esotericism, much beloved by Giovanni Torlonia Junior, the owl stands for the ability to see in darkness, exactly like the true sage who knows how to discern good from evil. What unifies the multiple architectural solutions of the place is certainly the gray shade of the roof. The Casina is structured on two floors; the interior is also richly decorated.

Perhaps less fairytale-like, but certainly no less impressive, is also the Theatre of Villa Torlonia, which is the final feature along the walk inside this park. Its history dates back to 1841 when Alessandro Torlonia commissioned it from architect Quintiliano Raimondi to celebrate his wedding to Teresa Colonna. A series of hiccups meant that work was not completed until 1874, but that did not stop it from being an authentic jewel. Just think that the interior was painted by Costantino Brumidi, who later emigrated to the United States and ended up decorating the American Parliament.

Casino Nobile in Villa Torlonia
Built in the Neoclassical style, it is now a museum.

From San Giovanni to Celio

The mother of Rome's churches

This itinerary begins at Rome Cathedral. Such is in fact the *Archbasilica of San Giovanni Laterano*. That this was for a long time the main church in the city can be immediately understood upon reading the epigraph that runs along the lintel of the façade and indicates *San Giovanni* as the mother and head of all churches. After all, it suffices to mention that it is dedicated to St. John, *The Apostle of God*, the author of the Fourth Gospel. One legend has him in Rome, martyred on 6 May 95, by a forced bath in a vat of boiling oil, from which he emerged without so much as a burn.

The church's façade, of a composite order with five tall, narrow arches that form a peristyle in front of the church, above which is a loggia gallery, is the work of Alessandro Galilei (1732-1735), whom the malicious tongues of the time judged to have friends in high places as he was the favourite architect of Cardinal Neri Corsini, himself a nephew of the current Pope Clement XII and Archpriest of the Basilica.

Having reached the entrance portico, we stop to admire the *Porta Santa* ('Holy Door'), the fifth from the left. It is the work of Flaviano Bodini and was inserted in place of the 14th-century one on the night of December 19-20, 2000, on the occasion of the last Jubilee officiated by John Paul II.

At the far end on our left, however, we can admire a statue of *Emperor Constantine*. It was the latter who wanted the construction of the Basilica here, which immediately lived through troubled years with constant plundering of its treasures, carried out by both the Visigoths of Alaric (410) and the Vandals of Janseric (455).

The interior of the Archbasilica of di San Giovanni with its nave. In the bac
ground is the ogival Tabernacle above the altar.

Once inside, we are faced with a five-arched structure that is the result of the rearrangement that took place in 1650 at the behest of Francesco Borromini. Above the nave runs a beautiful coffered ceiling that has triple attribution (Michelangelo, Daniele da Volterra, Pirro Ligorio) and was made in 1562 by the cabinetmaker Flaminio Boulanger.

Around us, we observe the imposing statues of the Twelve Apostles, set in as many niches. The arrangement project was also by Borromini. The Papal altar is surmounted by a splendid *Ogival Tabernacle*.

Inside it is possible to admire the precious *reliquary*, consisting of the holy heads of Peter and Paul. Unfortunately, it must be said that the *reliquary* is not an original one, but a 19th-century copy by Giuseppe Valadier. The tabernacle is supported by a cusped canopy. Under the altar is a *statue of St. John* that seems to have been put there to watch over the eternal sleep of Martin V.

In the background, the apse draws our attention. Its mosaic decoration is admirable. It depicts *The Triumph of the Cross*, and according to scholar Wilpert is an original mosaic from the Constantinian era. The last stop we make inside the basilica is in the right transept, where Luca Blasi's *Baroque Organ* towers. It is a work from 1590 and stands above the Basilica's northern entrance. We are amazed by its grandeur. Just think that the organ's central pipe is eight meters long and weighs two quintals. A revelation for music lovers: it is an F.

Holy Door of San Giovanni Laterano
It was installed, in place of the 14th-century one, on the occasion of the Jubilee of 2000.

The marble Altar of the Mithraeum of San Clemente. It is located on the thi
excavation level of the basilica and belonged to a Roman Domus.

Climbing up to the Caelian

Leaving the church, we turn to our left to ascend to Piazza San Giovanni. From here, walking down Via di San Giovanni, we come to Piazza di San Clemente, where stands the Basilica of the same name. This is a building that carries with it almost two thousand years of history through three distinct historical periods: the 2nd century, the 4th century, and the 12th century AD.

In fact, the basilica we can admire today is a structure drawn up ex novo by Pope Paschal II in the 12th century. Beneath it, virtually intact, is the earlier 4th-century basilica, under which are still preserved, as in a perfect system of Chinese boxes, the rooms of a 2nd-century Roman house, including the *Mithraeum*.

In the most recent building, at the height of the counterfaçade, is the Chapel of Santa Caterina, built by Cardinal Castiglioni during the 15th century and housing a cycle of frescoes that Vasari attributed to Masaccio. At this point we descend to the early Christian basilica below, erected in the 4th century in tribute to one of the first Popes of Christianity, Clement precisely. The latter is practically intact in its structure and preserves traces of frescoes that decorated the three naves, almost all of which had St. Clement's miracles as their theme. After that, we proceed down to the third level of excavations, namely the first floor of the Roman house, above which the two tiers of the basilica were built. The steady sound of water suggests that there was spring water flowing in the house, but more importantly, we can admire the remains of a *Mithraeum* consisting of a vestibule, triclinium and seats for initiates, as well as a coffered ceiling and a marble altar. The *Mithraeum* was the temple of the God Mithras, an Indo-European deity whose cult spread to Rome at the same time as Christianity.

Once outside, it is time to gain the summit of Caelian Hill, one

Apse of San Clemente with its mosaic Although uncertain, the work is dated to the pontificate of Paschal II (1099-1118).

Ancient Roman ruins at Villa Celimontana. Until the mid-16th century, the a: occupied by the villa was a vineyard.

of the seven mythical hills of this city. The oldest name for the Caelian would have been *Mons Querquetulanus* (Mount of the Oaks). Once reached, it is impossible to resist the temptation to enter *Villa Celimontana*. In the first half of the 16th century the area now occupied by the villa was a vineyard. In 1553 Giacomo Mattei, the same man already mentioned in connection with Piazza Mattei, bought the villa for 1,000 gold scudi, and Ciriaco Mattei, in 1580, decided to turn it into a villa. The architect Giacomo Del Duca, a disciple of Michelangelo, was entrusted with the building's construction and the landscaping of the surrounding park. The park was embellished with the Mattei family's remarkable collection of works of art.

Nothing can now be seen of the building's original appearance due to the constant restorations resulting from the frequent changes of ownership over time. The garden was finished by architects Giovanni and Domenico Fontana.

To conclude this itinerary we admire, just outside Villa Celimontana, the *Fontana della Navicella*, so called because of the shape of a Roman ship ('nave' in Italian). According to a legend La Navicella was found near the Colosseum and was allegedly a votive offering dedicated to Isis, the patroness of sailors. It is not known whether this ship was only restored or entirely made by Sansovino in 1519 due to severe damage to the original. What is certain is that the fountain was commissioned by Pope Leo X Medici, as attested by the coats of arms on the sides of the pedestal. At one time it was not in the position in which we see it today. The current arrangement dates back to 1931 and this change of position allows it to be fed by the Acqua Felice.

The Navicella
It was found near the Colosseum and restored by Sansovino in 1518-1519.

Via Luigi Petroselli

Via di S. Teodoro

Via di S Gregorio

Bocca della Verità

Circus Maximus

Roseto di Roma Capitale

Lungotevere Aventino

Giardino degli Aranci

Via delle Terme Deciane

M Circo Massin

Basilica di Santa Sabina sull'Aventino

Via di Santa Sabina

Clivio dei Publicii

United Nations

Piazza Giunone Regina

Buco della serratura dell'Ordine di Malta

Via di Sant'Alessio

Via di Porta Lavernale

Viale Aventino

Via Marmorata

Climbing the Aventine

A record-breaking construction

The majesty of the *Circus Maximus* marks the beginning of our journey up to the Aventine. According to tradition, it was founded by Tarquinius Priscus at the site of the Rape of the Sabine Women. It went on to expand over the centuries. It was in the 2nd century BC that it had its final, masonry structure, which made it the largest performance venue of all time: 600 meters long and 200 meters wide, with a capacity of 350,000 spectators. Here Augustus erected the *Obelisk of Ramesses II*, now in the centre of Piazza del Popolo. Constantius II instead had another Egyptian obelisk erected here, of *Thutmosis III*, from Thebes, which was moved during the 16th century to Piazza San Giovanni. The last races held here were in 549 at the behest of Totila, King of the Goths. During the Middle Ages it became the territory of fortifications, evidence of which today remains the small *Torre Frangipane*. A curiosity: in this tower stayed Jacopa de' Settesoli, a follower and friend of St. Francis, who was buried with him in Assisi.

It later became the site of executions. Now it is a long, grassy clearing, used in the past for collective celebrations after Roma's Scudetto (2001) and Italy's World Cup victory (2006). To this day it is also used for summer concerts by local and international rock stars.

Opposite the *Circus Maximus* stands the *Roseto Comunale*, Rome's *Rose Garden*. We are at the foot of the Aventine and the best time to visit it is certainly May, the month of roses. Although not very large (10,000 square m), it is considered one of the most beautiful in the world. It is split by Via della Murcia

Torre di Frangipane at Circus Maximus. A medieval fortification. Iacopa D
Settesoli, a follower and friend of St. Francis, stayed here.

into two sections, which have their backs to the Aventine. The largest section is on the left and houses a fascinating collection including botanical, ancient and modern roses. To the right, on the other hand, are the roses participating in the *Rome Grand Prix Competition*, one of the most prestigious in the world. Of course, all this takes place from May to early June.

The garden of lovers

Leaving the *Rose Garden*, we begin to enter the Aventine, immediately noticing the main feature of this hill: quietness. At a certain point in our ascent, we find on the right the *Giardino degli Aranci* (Garden of the Oranges). A small garden, popular with lovers and not. If you want to make the most of the view that this garden has to offer, it is ideal to reach its centre in Piazzale Fiorenzo Fiorentini, the latter being one of the most talented character actors of the post-WWII period. From this point, the Belvedere rock wall in front of us gives us the optical illusion of framing St. Peter's dome from below. It is precisely this point which offers the best view of the entire *Giardino degli Aranci*. In fact, if we reach the Belvedere, it is true that the view widens to include to our right the *Quirinale* and to our left the district of *Monteverde al Gianicolo*, but it is also true that the traffic of the Lungotevere below, often clogged with cars, creates a background noise that in a way breaks the spell of this garden.

Roseto Comunale
A glimpse of the rose garden. It rises at the foot of the Aventine Hill.

Once back on the road, we immediately find the *Church of Santa Sabina*. It dates from early Christian times and was built in 425 by a priest, Peter of Illyria, on the site of an old house of the matron Sabina. The fact that the church was dedicated to her is attributable to a misunderstanding: the matron was confused with the Umbrian

The interior of Santa Sabina all'Aventino. It is bare in the tradition of early Christian churches. It was built in 425 AD.

saint, whom legend has it was martyred under Hadrian. The *Portal*, carved in wood, belongs to the early period of the basilica. The interior is bare, as per early Christian tradition. It must be said that this original arrangement is due to the 20th-century restoration ordered by Munoz, who eliminated the Baroque decorations that were the result of the restoration by Domenico Fontana (1587) and Borromini (1643). The three naves are divided by columns from the Temple of Juno Regina, which used to stand nearby. The basin of the large semi-circular apse was frescoed by Taddeo Zuccari with Jesus, the apostles and saints buried in the basilica. Taddeo, brother of Federico, also a painter, was a noted Italian Mannerist. Two interesting facts about him: he died on 1 September 1566, him having been born on 1 September thirty-seven years earlier, and was buried in the Pantheon next to Raphael Sanzio, who was his Ideal Master and who-ironically enough-also died at the age of thirty-seven.

Church of Sant'Alessio

Leaving Santa Sabina, next door we find the *Church of Sant'Alessio*. Actually, its real name is *Basilica of Santi Bonifacio e Alessio*. Before entering, let us dwell on the two saints it is dedicated to. Boniface, martyred in Tarsus in Cilicia, was venerated here on the Aventine since the 7th century. As for the more highly regarded St. Alexius, however, the most credited of the legends that arose about him says that after the 4th century Alexius, son of the wealthy Euphemianus, a resident of the Aventine, on the night of his marriage to a young noblewoman, feeling called to a life of piety, left his home and family to go and preach in Edessa. He stayed there for 17 years, earning a huge reputation as a saint. At that point, in disguise, he decided to

The mascaron
Fontana del Giardino degli aranci. The marble mascaron was carved by Giacomo Della Porta.

View of St. Peter's from the Keyhole of Rome. We are in the garden of the Grand
Priory of the Order of the Knights of Malta.

return to his own home, as a servant of servants, to live another 17 years of penance.

At his death a multitude of people flocked to his bedside, summoned by a miraculous ringing of bells, and in his hand the Pope found a writing illustrating his entire life. Thus it was that in 986 the Basilica of San Bonifacio, whose origin dated back to the 5th century, was also dedicated to the latter saint, who shortly ousted him as the main titleholder.

Beyond the front courtyard, we can admire the 18th-century façade, inspired by that of Santi Apostoli, under which a portico puts us in front of the stunning Cosmatesque portal, a remnant of the building commissioned by Honorius III in the 13th century. Inside the church, the most famous work of art is in the *Tabernacle* of the *Capella del Santissimo Sacramento* and is the *Madonna di Sant'Alessio*.

This is a tempera on canvas, datable between the 12th and 13th centuries, which depicts the *Virgin without the Child*, facing to one side, with her bust slightly bent, one hand forward and the other up in a gesture commonly understood to be one of intercession for those who have no hope except in her. It is no accident that the other appellation of this Virgin is Our Lady of Intercession.

Outside Sant'Alessio, we quickly reach the *Buco di Roma* ('The Keyhole of Rome') the terminus of this walk of ours. It is located on Piazza dei Cavalieri di Malta and is the keyhole of the gate of the Grand Priory of the Order of the Knights of Malta. If we approach the hole, we can see, in a gallery perspective shaped by an avenue of specially trimmed plants, the Dome of St. Peter's framed as if in a painting. A truly unique view.

The "Keyhole" of Rome
Detail of the entrance gate of the Grand Priory of the Order of the Knights of Malta: it is the 'Keyhole' of Rome.

Piazza dei Cavalieri
di Malta

Viale Aventino

Via Luca della Robbia

Via Marmorata

Parco
della Resistenza

Viale della
Piramide Cestia

Piazza
Testaccio

Via Manuzio

Via Volta

Tomba
di Keats

Porta
San Paolo

M Piramide

Piramide
di Caio Cestio

Cimitero
Acattolico

Via Ostiense

Tomba di
Gramsci

Rome war
Cemetery

Via di Monte
Testaccio

Roma Ostiense

Testaccio and the Non-Catholic Cemetery

The resting place of poets and artists

There is an unsuspected magical place in the shadow of Rome's Piramide Cestia and it is called *Cimitero Acattolico di Testaccio* ('Non-Catholic Cemetery'), also known as *Degli Inglesi*. It was created during the 1700s to allow for the burial of foreigners stationed in Rome who did not practice the Catholic religion and therefore could not be buried in traditional cemeteries.

Let us go and discover it.

The entrance is on Via Caio Cestio. As soon as we cross the entrance, we head to our left reaching the part behind the walls, called *Cimitero Vecchio* ('Old Cemetery'), where Protestants were buried. As we enter we realize that the air we breathe is not the mournful air of any cemetery, but romantic and quiet. It is as if the spirits of the poets and artists buried here give this place the aura of an oasis of eternity, amidst centuries-old pines and cypresses, wild roses and camellias.

Who was the first Protestant buried here?

One William Arthur, a Protestant physician from Edinburgh, in exile in Rome for supporting James III Stuart. Burial was by Papal concession *"to bury him beside the Sepulcher of Cestius, within the walls."* Thus it was that the Non-Catholic became the cemetery for foreigners on the Grand Tour. Initially, there were no walls, and flocks grazed among the tombs. The only protection was offered by holly shrubs. In 1821 Pius IX granted a new adjoining plot of land, which would become the Cimitero Nuovo ('New Cemetery'), and in addition, a protective moat was dug around the old one.

In the Cimitero Vecchio, where we are, it is proper to pause in front of the grave of Keats, whose affairs we discussed in the chapter on the Tridente. This bears the following epitaph:

Monte dei Cocci in Testaccio. It is an artificial hill composed of numerous laye
of Roman Amphora shards

"Here lies one whose name was written on the water."

Above it the simple wording 'Young English Poet'.

When Oscar Wilde passed through these parts, he came to the grave to pay his respects to the unfortunate English poet, here remaining several minutes in recollection.

It is impossible not to notice in front of us, beyond the *grave of Keats*, the imposing bulk of the Piramide Cestia. The latter has a curious history and bears the date of the 1st century BC, when Caius Cestius, an important politician in Rome, wanted a pyramid as a funerary monument. That was the period during which wealthy Romans were fascinated by Oriental tastes. Caius Cestius decided to have it built outside the city, along a consular road, L'Ostiense, which connected Rome with the port of Ostia Antica. Its construction took 330 days. The structure is portentous: 37 meters high with a square base of about 30 meters on each side. It was originally surrounded by four columns and an enclosure built of tuff blocks. Today only two columns, unearthed in 1656, are visible. The burial chamber is a small room, in contrast to the grandeur of the structure, but features walls entirely covered with frescoes. Its appearance, somewhat original, made it become a must-see stop on the 18th and 19th-century *Grand Tour*.

Piramide Cestia Dated 1st cent. BC, it was commissioned by the politician Caius Cestius as his own funerary monument.

Moving to the new part of the cemetery, it is fitting to pause at the grave of the poet Shelley, who died in a shipwreck in the Tyrrhenian Sea and was found with Keats' poems in his pocket. The body was identified by Byron and moved here. Very poetic is his epigraph taken from Shakespeare's The Tempest:

"Nothing about him dissolves but undergoes a marine metamorphosis to become something rich and strange."

A cat watches over a grave in Testaccio's Non-Catholic Cemetery. The feline colony that populates the cemetery's alleys is substantial.

The poet was cremated, but according to legend, his wife Mary, the author of *Frankenstein*, had his heart rescued from the flames so that he could be buried with her in England. True? Who knows, certainly very Gothic.

In this quiet place, in addition to great foreign poets and artists, there is also room for distinguished Italians. Famous is the grave of Antonio Gramsci, which also has the distinction of containing a Latin grammar error in the engraving: *Cinera Antonii Gramscii*, when it would have been correct to write *Cineres Antonii Gramscii*. The anti-fascist philosopher was buried here by virtue of his marriage to Giulia Schucht, a Soviet of Orthodox confession.

On the writers' side are Emilio Lussu, Carlo Emilio Gadda, and Andrea Camilleri. The tomb of Montalbano's dad is easily identifiable thanks to personalized signage and by the fact that it is always embellished with small gifts, including packs of cigarettes and arancini, which fans who come here on pilgrimage never fail to bring. Just think that the young Andrea Camilleri, a student of directing at the National Academy of Dramatic Art in the late 1940s, discovered the beauties of Rome while walking at night and especially in the company of the painter Mario Mafai, whom he met by chance in a bar in Piazza del Popolo where Camilleri went to dine with a cappuccino. Different times, never to be repeated.

Grave of Gramsci
The engraving *Cinera Antonii Gramscii* contains a Latin grammatical error.

Circonvallazione Ostiense

Via Cristoforo Colombo

Piazza Eugenio Biffi

Piazza Giovanni da Lucca

Albergo rosso

Piazza Michele da Carbonara

Via da cesinale

Via Magnaghi

Carlotta Fountain

Lovers' Staircase

Piazza Nicola Longobardi

Bar dei Cesaroni

Via Vittorio Cumberti

Teatro Garbatella

Via Francesco Passino

Church of San Francesco Saverio

Church of San Filippo Neri

Largo delle Sette Chiese

Via delle Sette Chiese

Via Macinghi Strozzi

Via della Villa Lucini

Garbatella

Between quiet pathways and film sets

It is one of the areas in Rome that has seen its appeal grow the most in recent years, so much so that it is counted among the must-see neighbourhoods the moment one sets foot in Rome on a visit. It is the perfect example of the suburbs gaining centrality in the city's urban fabric.

A walk through *Garbatella* must necessarily begin at Piazza Benedetto Brin, the spot where the neighbourhood was officially born on February 18, 1920, with the foundation stone laid by King Victor Emmanuel III.

Why the name *Garbatella*? There are three hypothesis. The first sees the name derived from the Garbata crops, typical of the hills that characterized the landscape before the development of the district. The second hypothesis refers to the particular amenity of the place. The third is the most credited and refers to the presence in the neighbourhood of an inn whose hostess had extraordinarily kind and polite manners, so much so that she was named *Garbata Ostella* ('kind hostess'). The Osteria was located on Via delle Sette Chiese. The dwellings were built to house the families of the workers engaged in the industrial works of the Ostiense Quarter, who were later joined by the evacuees of the demolitions around the Area Sacra of Largo Argentina and Piazza Montanara, housed here in the so-called suburban hotels.

Architecturally, the inspiration was that of the English garden city and the logic of the allotments. It began by using the so-called Roman Baroque, which was followed by Futurist rationalism. Strolling through the old *Garbatella*, one really has the feeling of being in an autonomous village within the city. A stop

The staircase that stands next to the Carlotta Fountain. It is known as 'The Lo ers' Staircase.'

at Piazza Nicola Longobardi, in front of the *Scoletta*, the name by which the 'Luigi Luzzatti' Kindergarten School is known, is a must. It is an old villa of the papal nobility dating back to the 1500s. The original name was Villa Rosselli and was in turn derived from a 1st-century Roman villa. Today's structure is the work of architect Innocenzo Sabatini, who designed this children school between 1919 and 1922. The building was also portrayed in the film *Totò and Marcellino* and in a late-1990s Italian TV drama, Caro Maestro.

After all, this neighbourhood has always had a very strong connection with postwar Italian cinema and television. Some scenes of the film *Le ragazze di piazza di Spagna* were filmed here, the 'Povero ma Bello' Maurizio Arena was born here, the bar of the series *I Cesaroni* is here, and also here you can admire a beautiful mural dedicated to Alberto Sordi and his films. By the way, there are many examples of *Street Art* scattered among the streets of *Garbatella*.

One of the places in the heart of the neighbourhood is certainly *Fontana Carlotta*. Alongside it begins the so-called *Scala degli Innamorati* ('Lovers' Staircase'), a favourite meeting point for couples. Innocenzo Sabatini was also the architect of the aforementioned *suburban hostels*, of which the most noteworthy is the *Albergo Rosso*. The latter has a very special story to tell. The clock which surmounts it for a very long time stood still on the hour of the bombing of Rome in World War II, 11:25 to be precise. Therefore it was long considered the emblem of the people's resistance against the war.

Bar of the Cesaroni
A well-known hangout in the neighbourhood, especially after the airing of the TV drama of the same name.

Useful Info

CHURCHES

Santa Maria Maggiore
Piazza di Santa Maria Maggiore
Opening times: 7-18:45
Tel: 06/69886800

San Giovanni in Laterano
Piazza di San Giovanni Laterano 4
Opening times: 7:00-18:30
Tel: 06/69886433

San Lorenzo in Panisperna
Via Panisperna 90
Tel: 06/646535573-06/46535574
To arrange a visit please contact the
numbers provided

Santi Domenico e Sisto
Largo Angelicum 1
Open on Saturday from 15:00 -18:00;
Advance booking required: 06/67021-
06/6702341

Sant'Andrea al Quirinale
Via del Quirinale 30
Tuesday to Sunday: 9:00-12:00,
15:00-18:00; Tel: 06/4819399

San Carlino alle Quattro Fontane
Via del Quirinale 23
Monday to Saturday: 10:00-13:00
Sunday: 12:00-13:00; Tel: 06/488361

Santa Maria della Vittoria
Via Venti Settembre 17
8:30-12:00, 15:00-18:00
Tel: 42740571

San Clemente
Via Labicana 95
Advance booking required:
06/7740021

Santa Maria in Domenica alla Navicella
Via della Navicella 10
Tel: 06/84384209 – To arrange a visit
please contact the numbers provided

Chiesa del Gesù
Via degli Astalli 16
Monday to Saturday: 7:30-12:30,
17:00-19:30; Sunday and holidays: 7:45-
13:45, 17:00-20:00; Tel: 06/697001

Sant'Ignazio
Via del Caravita 8/a
Opening Times: 9-20; Tel: 06/6794406

Sant'Andrea della Valle
Corso Vittorio Emanuele II
Monday to Saturday: 15:00-19:30,
Sunday: 8.30-19:30; Tel: 06/6861330

Sant'Ivo alla Sapienza
Corso Rinascimento 40
Open on Sunday from 9:00 – 12:00.

Santi Ambrogio e Carlo al Corso
Via del Corso 437
Opening times: 7:00-19:00; Tel:
06/68192527

Sant'Agnese in Agone
Piazza Navona
Tuesday to Sunday: 9:00-12:30,
15:30–19:00;
Tel: 06/68192134

San Luigi dei Francesi
Piazza San Luigi dei Francesi
Opening times: 10:00-12:30,
15:00 – 19:00
Tel: 06/688271

Santa Maria in Montesanto
Piazza del Popolo 18
Monday to Friday: 10:00-12:00,
17:00-20:00; Saturday: 10:00-17:00
Sunday: 11:00-13:30

Santa Maria dei Miracoli
Via del Corso 528
Opening times: 7:00-12:30,
16:00-19:30
Tel: 06/3610250

Santa Maria della Pace
Arco della Pace 5
Opening times: 9:30-18:00
Tel: 06/68804038

St Peter's
Piazza San Pietro
Opening times: 7:00-18:30
Tel: 06/6982

San Pietro in Montorio
Piazza San Pietro in Montorio 2
For visits contact 060608

Santa Maria in Trastevere
Piazza Santa Maria in Trastevere
Opening times: 7:30-21:00
Tel: 06/5814802

Sant'Angelo in Pescheria
Via della Tribuna di Campitelli 6
To arrange a visit please contact
06/68801819

Santa Maria del Popolo
Piazza del Popolo
Opening times: Sunday to Thursday:
7:00-12:30, 16:00-19:00;
Friday and Saturday: 7:30-19:00
Tel: 060608

Santa Sabina
Piazza Pietro d'Illiria 1
Tel: 06/579401 – To arrange a visit
please contact the numbers provided.

Santi Bonifacio e Alessio
Piazza di Sant'Alessio 23s
Monday to Sunday: 10:00-12:30,
15:30-19:00 – Saturday and Sunday:
9:00-12:30, 15:30-19:00; Morning:
6:30-12:30; Afternoon: 16:00-18:30;
Sunday: 6:30-13:00

MUSEUMS

Museo storico dei Bersaglieri
Piazza di Porta Pia
Tel: 06/486723 – To arrange a visit
please contact the number provided.

Casino Nobile di Villa Torlonia
Via Nomentana 70
Tuesday to Sunday: 9:00-19:00
Tel: 060608

Casina delle Civette
Via Nomentana 70
Tuesday to Sunday: 9:00-19:00
Tel: 060608

Galleria Nazionale d'Arte Moderna
Viale delle Belle Arti 131
Tuesday to Sunday: 9:00-19:00
Tel: 06322981

Museo Carlo Bilotti
Viale Fiorello La Guardia 6
Tuesday to Friday: 10:00-16:00
Saturday and Sunday: 10:00-14:00
Tel: 060608

Museo Pietro Canonica
Viale Pietro Canonica 2
Tuesday to Sunday: 10:00-16:00
Tel: 060608

Galleria Borghese
Piazzale Scipione Borghese 5
Tuesday to Sunday: 9:00-19:00
Tel: 06/67233753

Casa di Goethe
Via del Corso 18
Tuesday to Sunday: 10:00-18:00
Tel: 06/32650412

Keats-Shelley Memorial House
Piazza di Spagna 26
Daily from: 10:00-13:00,
14:00-18:00; Tel: 06/6784235

Ara Pacis
Lungotevere in Augusta
Tuesday to Sunday: 9:30-19:30 –
Tel: 060608

Palazzo Braschi (Museo di Roma)
Piazza San Pantaleo 10
- Piazza Navona 2
Tuesday to Sunday: 10-19;
Tel: 060608

Musei Vaticani
Viale Vaticano 51
Monday to Thursday: 8:00-18:30 –
Friday and Saturday: 8:00-22:30
Closed on Sudday; Tel: 06/69884676

Palazzo Corsini
(Galleria Nazionale d'Arte Antica)
Via della Lungara 10
Tel: 06/68802323

Palazzo Barberini
(Galleria Nazionale d'Arte Antica)
Via delle Quattro Fontane 13
Tuesday to Sunday: 10:00-18:00
Tel: 06/4814591

Museo Ebraico
Via Catalana
Sunday to Thursday: 10:00-17:00
Friday: 9:00-14:00; Tel: 06/68400661

Musei Capitolini
Piazza del Campidoglio 1
Tuesday to Sunday: 9:30-19:30
Tel: 060608

SITES OF INTEREST

Torre delle Milizie
Salita del Grillo 37
Opening times: 9:00-17:00

Villa Torlonia
Via Nomentana 70
From 1 October to 31 March:
7:00-19:00; From 1 April to 30
September: 7:00-20:30

Teatro Torlonia
Via Lazzaro Spallanzani 1/a
Tel: 06/44230693

Villa Celimontana
Via della Navicella - Piazza SS.
Giovanni e Paolo
From 7:00 to sunset

Cimitero Acattolico
Via Caio Cestio 6
Saturday: 9:00-17:00, Sunday:
9:00-13:00
Tel: 06/5741900

Piramide Cestia
Via Raffaele Persichetti
Tel: 06/39967700

Teatro Palladium
Piazza Bartolomeo Romano 8
Tel: 06/57332772

Moby dick
Biblioteca Hub Culturale
Via Edgardo Ferrati 3/a
Monday to Saturday: 10:00-21:00
Sunday: 10:00-14:00
Tel: 06/49701717

Villa Borghese
Open 24/7

Gigi Proietti Globe Theatre
Largo Acqua Felix
Infoline: 338 91104467 – Open
from late June to October

Casa del Cinema
Largo Marcello Mastroianni 1
Tel: 060608

Pantheon
Piazza della Rotonda
Monday to Saturday: 8:30-19:15
Sunday: 9:00-17:45

Atelier Canova Tadolini
Via del Babuino 150/a
Tuesday to Sunday: 8:00-24:00
Tel: 06/32110702

Complesso del Vittoriano
Via di San Pietro in Carcere
Monday to Thursday: 9:30-19:30
Friday and Saturday: 9:30-22
Sunday: 9:30-20:30
Tel: 06/6780664

Antico Caffè Greco
Via dei Condotti 80
Open daily from 9-22
Tel: 06/6791700

Babingtons
Piazza di Spagna 23
Wednesday to Monday: 10:00-23:30
Closed on Tuesday; Tel: 06/6786027

Castel Sant'Angelo
Lungotevere Castello 10
Tuesday to Sunday: 9-19:30
Tel: 06/6819111

Spezieria di Santa Maria della Scala
Piazza della Scala
Monday to Saturday: 8:30-20:30
Tel: 06/5806217

Teatro Argentina
Largo di Torre Argentina 52
Tel: 06/684000314

Orto Botanico di Roma
Largo Cristina di Svezia 23/a
Open daily: 9:00-18:30
Tel: 06/49917107

Villa Doria Pamphilj
Via di San Pancrazio
Open daily: 8:00-20:00

Index of Names and Places

Churches

Popes

Piazze and vie

Index

Printed in July 2023
on behalf of Edizioni Intra Moenia
by Vulcanica Srl